# GHOST TRAILS
## TO CALIFORNIA

# GHOST TRAILS
## TO CALIFORNIA

by Thomas H. Hunt / Photographs by Thomas H. Hunt and Robert V. H. Adams

*With Selected Excerpts from Emigrant Journals*

**IMAGES OF AMERICA SERIES**

AMERICAN WEST PUBLISHING COMPANY
PALO ALTO · CALIFORNIA

*To Lucretia, who was ever with us . . .*

# Acknowledgments:

The author would like to express his sincere thanks and appreciation to George Stewart for kindly reading the text and offering his most instructive criticisms. Any reader interested in pursuing further the fascinating story of the emigration to California will find no better historical survey of the topic than Mr. Stewart's *The California Trail*. Of course, Mr. Stewart is not responsible for the author's shortcomings in the area of either facts or interpretation.

The base map on pages 6-7 is reprinted, by permission of Xerox College Publishing, from an original by Erwin Raisz in Wallace T. Atwood's *Physiographic Provinces of North America*, © copyright Ginn and Company, 1940. Film for the base maps appearing in the Portfolio of Maps on pages 263-285 was supplied by the United States Geological Survey.

All illustrations appearing in the introductory section are by J. Goldsborough Bruff, sketched on his journey to the West in 1849.

**Other Images of America Series Books:**
LIVING WATER
THIS LIVING EARTH
STEINBECK COUNTRY
ANASAZI: *Ancient People of the Rock*
MYSTIQUE OF THE MISSIONS

FIRST EDITION

© Copyright 1974, AMERICAN WEST PUBLISHING COMPANY. Printed in the United States of America. All rights reserved. This book, or parts thereof, may not be reproduced in any form without written permission of the publisher.

Library of Congress Card Number 74-79041

ISBN: regular casebound edition, 0-910118-56-6; deluxe edition, 0-910118-57-4

# CONTENTS

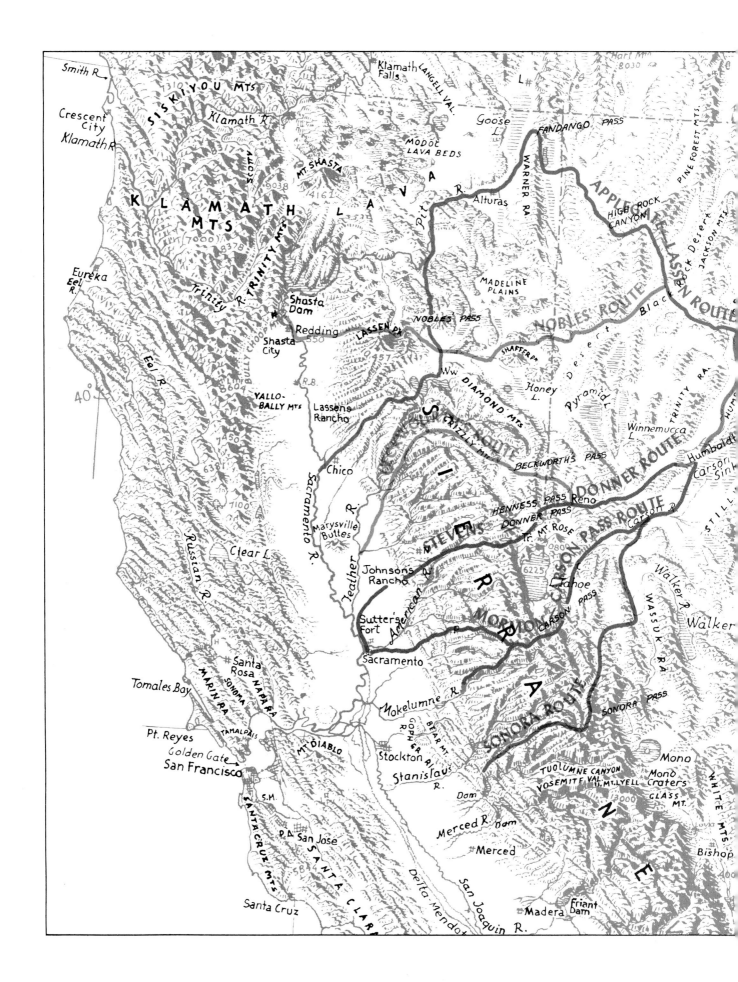

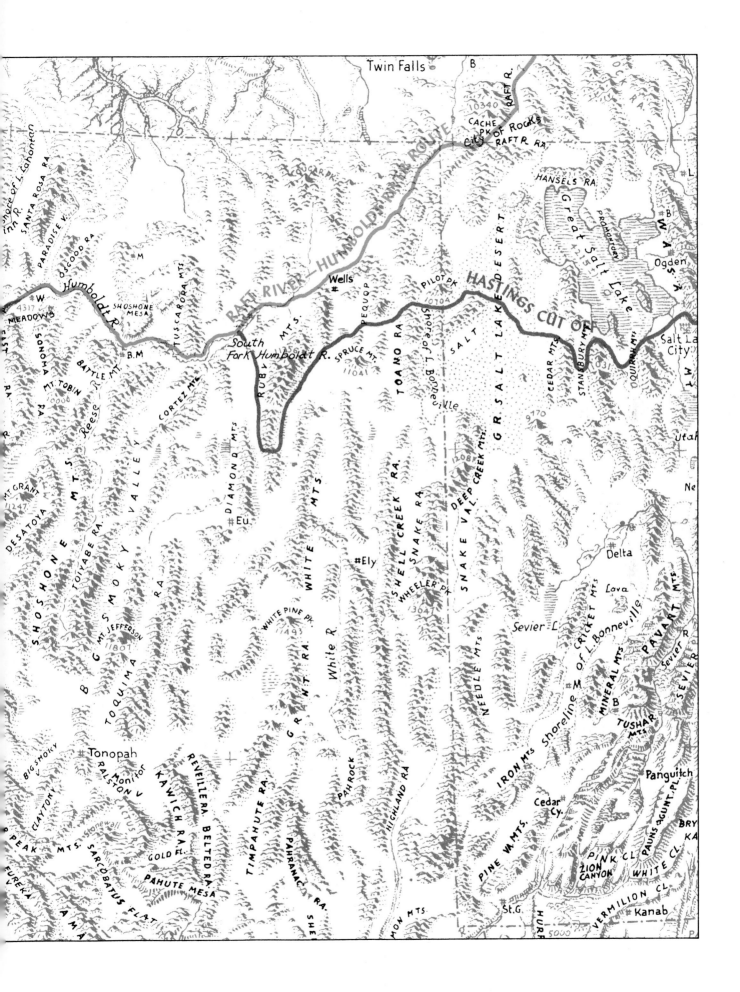

The Raft River Approach

The Hastings Cutoff

The Humboldt River Route

# The Applegate-Lassen Route

The Mormon-Carson Route

The Stevens-Donner Route

# PREFACE

One cannot spend as many years as the author has camping and back-packing in the high country of the Sierra Nevada without quite soon and surprisingly often coming across a notation on a topographical map, or a granite-and-bronze marker, or a resin-beaded carving on an ancient blaze on a gnarled pine tree, or a faint trace up a prodigious mountain slope, all of which echo the passing of the California-bound emigrants. I suppose a general curiosity about the how and why and whither began with such scattered and fragmentary encounters with these testaments to that epic migration, and from the ever-widening pursuit over the years since of the ramifications of that incipient curiosity, there finally evolved the idea for a photo essay on the California Trail.

The need for such an effort certainly exists. While the written record is now safely preserved, the visual record—the record on the land—is only fragilely preserved and has been recorded only poorly and piecemeal. This book does not presume to be a definitive, encyclopedic record of historical facts and figures concerning this particular portion of the great westward movement in America (this is a field already well covered by the professional historian); it is rather intended to be a book of selected good readings which strives to catch the mood and flavor of those bygone times, which hopes to be an evocation of the trials and tribulations, the hopes and fears, the moments of humor and pleasure and sorrow and despair of those who journeyed across the deserts and over the mountains of the California Trail as they have come down to us in the words of the emigrants themselves. And to these words, distilled from contemporary journals and diaries, and passed on to us through the efforts of many scholars, Van Adams and I have attempted to add through photographs the dimension of a rich visual experience of the trail.

Early in this endeavor it was decided to make every effort to follow out the emigrant routes as accurately as they could be established from contemporary emigrant journals, maps, and guides, as well as from the various subsequent scholarly studies and modern topographical maps. Each of these fields of study has proved helpful in its own way but also ever more addictive, and what started so casually to be at most a summer or two of pleasant rambling in familiar places has somehow turned out to be a serious project of six years' duration and extending to some of the least known and seldom visited regions of our country. Over the years it has meant a great deal of research and reading, a great deal of puzzling over maps and journal entries, and some twenty thousand miles of driving and hiking. It has often been exasperating, occasionally tedious, sometimes downright unpleasant, but it has never been uninteresting or unrewarding.

Often we have stood at some point along the trail that we or others had established to our satisfaction to be correct and asked ourselves: "Now why did they come this way, and where did they go from here?" As to the why of it, we may never know for certain because some of these routes seem to us, from our present vantage point in time and with our modern topographical references, to be capricious and sometimes even foolish. As to the where, only careful examination on foot and a reversion to the realities and logic of nineteenth-century travel can provide an answer.

The first thing one learns is that one certainly cannot hope to be too successful in predicting the course of a wagon-and-oxen track on the basis of an automobile-and-gas-station mentality. The prerequisite energy for our means of mechanical locomotion comes ever so conveniently to us these days through the ubiquitous gas pump at the side of a freeway. In emigrant days, the means of transport had to travel to its fuel supply, and this fundamental difference in our mechanical—as opposed to their animal—transportation serves to explain a great deal. Basically, all decisions as to routing had to take into consideration the availability of grass and water for the stock. After these two essentials were provided for, there could be further consideration as to destination and time.

But even taking these factors into account, the question still often presents itself: "Why didn't they just veer off to the right up that other valley and take what to us would seem to be the easier, shorter, more logical route?" Beyond the supposition that such random choices of trail-making must owe a lot to chance and ignorance and habit, it is probably best just to accept the facts of a given trail for what they are, with perhaps the outside hope that someday a still unknown manuscript may come to light and add a tasty morsel to the diet of us who delight in supping on such exotic footnotes and historical minutiae. After all, it is such unexplained vagaries that add the titillation of mystery and the spice of challenge to the job of trail-tracing.

Setting aside, therefore, all such futile, albeit tantalizing speculations, we must return to the task that we set for ourselves when undertaking this book, and that was simply to follow out and present with as much accuracy as possible the record of all the major segments which went to make up the whole of the California Trail. We cannot claim to have established beyond all doubt the exact, foot-by-foot route of each one of these branches, but we do claim to be reasonably close. Since those first few California-bound wagons turned south and west away from the faint traces of a horse trail to Oregon, in the vicinity of Sheep Rock on the Bear River in 1841, there have been just too many changes wrought upon the land by man to permit more precision than that. Cities and towns have grown up all along the way; farms have been laid out, forests felled, streams dammed, railroads and great freeways cut through valleys and across mountains. Indeed, when one stops and considers the immense physical changes made in the landscape by the descendants of those early emigrants, the miracle is not that there are so few traces left to be found, but that there are so many.

For the fact is that, despite the constant inroads of civilization, there are still miles and miles of emigrant traces left to follow out if one has the mind to do so. There are desert valleys where one can stand waist-high in the pungent sagebrush and see the ruts of wagon wheels curve up a draw and out of sight behind a screen of piñon pines. There are alkali flats and sandy wastes where rusty barrel hoops and crockery shards and the bleached bones of oxen can yet be found. There are high mountain passes where—with only the slightest exercise of one's imagination—one can picture the ragged forty-niner, ebullient at having reached the final summit of the Sierra, letting his pack mule nibble at the wind-shriveled grasses while he takes out the small canteen of good old "Kaintuck" whiskey that he had so carefully hoarded and preserved all across the endless plains and deserts just to have it at this moment of personal triumph to toast his own good fortune, courage, and perseverance while scrawling his name in lampblack or whitewash among all the others on the granite boulder at the side of the trail. There are alpine valleys where one can conjure up images of travel-battered wagons drawn up beside the gurgling, crystalline waters of snowmelt streams, while beyond them the bony oxen fairly groaned with pleasure and contentment in swales of knee-deep mountain grass, grass still green and succulent even in the months of late autumn. One can hear the metallic bite of the ax into pitchy, resonant trunks of whitebark pines and the voices of children happily at play across the meadow, and smell the salt pork bubbling with freshly picked wild onions in the blackened kettle over a crackling fire. And one can see the pioneer father take out his whittling knife and carve his name and the year of passing into the still fresh blaze on a convenient tree—a testament to achievement, a writing under the bark for future generations to ponder upon when they, too, pass through these meadows, not driven by any imperative need to conquer, not forced to prevail or perish, but merely seeking to enjoy this wilderness and perchance to find a bit of personal renewal.

Yes, miraculously enough, these spots are still there to be seen and experienced by those who find such things stimulating, even moving. They are special places, places full of poignancy and meaning. They were places won only after tough, brutal miles, and they were won by a tough, resilient people.

These emigrants weren't angels, they weren't martyrs, they weren't some special breed of demi-gods, and it would be wrong to picture them as such. But no one of any sensibility can walk even a few miles on a blistering September day out across the Forty Mile Desert beyond the great Sink of the Humboldt, or crawl up those final five hundred feet above Red Lake to the first crest of the Sierra on the Carson Pass Trail, and not know that they were indeed a special, extraordinarily tough breed of people, taking part in one of the truly heroic events in human history. They bridged a hostile continent and rounded out a continental nation, and they did it step by dust-filled, unglamorous step.

If they had to throw away everything of value and sentiment from their past back in the States in order to win out over desert sands, they did it; regretful but resolute, they did it. If they had to tear down a wagon completely and carry it piece by piece to the top of a mountain, where it was reassembled to continue the journey, well, they did just that; and such heartrending decisions and toilsome efforts were the full measure of their ultimate triumph, too. Theirs was a record of fortitude and determination and truly monumental achievement.

But beyond the epic and the heroic, these were simply *people*—a people hard-tempered and hard-tested by times to which they were usually, but not always, equal. They laughed, they cried, they prayed, they profaned, they were cruel and selfish, they were compassionate and generous, they despaired, they exalted, and sometimes they just grabbed up their fiddles and danced the Devil into submission under their dusty heels simply because the feeling to dance was upon them and they'd be goddamned if they'd let that hellish trail get the best of them.

This is a book about people and the land through which they passed in seeking a new life. Our two fundamental goals in compiling it were to choose quotations that show people as people and photographs that show the land as it *was*. For this reason, the text may be a little misleading, since it is a selected anthology of the most literate and readable passages from among a great number of emigrant writings. The reader should keep in mind that the majority of extant journals and diaries are little more than briefly annotated mileage records, the entries terse and laconic and highly uninteresting. This is to be expected, of course, among any sizable sampling of such records. Journals and diaries were kept by only a minority of the emigrants to begin with, and from among this restricted number we have purposely excluded the writings of those who were neither stimulated by their surroundings nor especially stimulating in their own thoughts and observations. Added to this sort of selective bias in the sampling is the further fact that by the time the emigrants had entered on the California Trail and taken up this last, most grueling leg of their two-thousand-mile odyssey, both humans and animals were worn to a frazzle by their unending succession of daily ordeals. They were mentally tired and often physically weakened from too little food or too restricted a diet.

It is really only the occasional gifted person who rises above the concerns of day-to-day trivia to give us the fresh insight, the poetic expression, the incisive and memorable phrase, the emotional substance of the experience. It is from the writings of these rare people that this book is primarily drawn, and it would certainly be inaccurate on both historical and human grounds to leave the reader with the impression that the average emigrant was ever so observant, always so receptive, always so perceptive.

Nor are the events memorialized in the diaries completely reflective of all those days when tedium and drudgery prevailed and there simply wasn't anything picturesque or momentous to record.

And yet, it is fully hoped and expected that these excerpts—even specially chosen as they are—do catch the real substance and mood of the emigrants' collective experiences along the California Trail. It is not intended to be an ordinary view, certainly, but it is intended that, taken in sum, it adds up to the view in common.

One final word about the photographs and the difficulties they have presented. There were two fundamental concepts for the photographic effort. The first was to present the country through which the emigrant trails wound just as close to the way it appeared to the emigrant as was possible. The second hope was to photograph it at approximately the same time of year as the emigrant would have viewed it. Pursuant to the first goal, we have purposely excluded any scenes that show the subsequent intrusion of man-made artifacts or improvements. This has often proved to be most difficult and exasperating, for as a general rule the emigrants succeeded in establishing arteries of travel and corridors of settlement which have been expanding ever since. The ubiquitous scars of industry and commerce, transportation, communication, and recreation are not easy to avoid. We have, however, determinedly avoided them and occasionally have been hard-pressed for adequate coverage because of it (one has only to drive the Truckee River Canyon to appreciate this problem). It has required returning again and again to certain crucial localities to get just the right shot, but we consider the results to be most gratifying and certainly worth the effort. Concerning the second criterion—the seasonableness of the pictures—we have not always been as successful. It has just proved to be impossible, even given the spread of years involved in this effort, to get to every area along the divergent routes at just the right time of year. We can only plead that, while not always exactly correlated with journal dates, we have striven to be at least plausibly close.

In the process of compiling this book we cannot claim to have discovered anything of startling historical moment; we do not even have an exciting little tidbit of western memorabilia to chronicle. Although we have made some very minor corrections as to the courses of some trails, it must be fully accepted that at this time in the study of the California Trail there are not any outstanding disputes as to routes and historical intentions left for us to attempt to settle.

The value to us of this effort lies rather in another direction; it lies in the direction of personal satisfaction. We have seen rare and beautiful country that only a handful of people even know exists within the public domain. We have, over the years, collected a few rusty barrel hoops, a corroded nail or two, an occasional bottle, and a cupful of shards of emigrant crockery. We must also admit to having on occasion experienced that sort of perverse pleasure (which must be allowed those of us who become too interested in narrow historical pursuits) which arises from finding out that the professional scholars have made some mistakes concerning the route followed by a particular journalist. And through it all, we have been impressed, and deeply so, by the will and vitality and courage of the emigrants, and we have constantly marveled at their physical endurance and accomplishments.

When one looks back on all of this, one might be inclined to say that these little satisfactions and petty triumphs were small indeed—perhaps too small to repay one for all the time and effort expended. It is not so, and I can only hope that somehow the alchemy of words may work some little magic on my readers' imaginations and let them join me in a very special sort of feeling.

It is a feeling that is hard to put precisely into words. It is a feeling that one gets in the middle of the desert, in that absolute stillness which is always to be found there but which seems most marvelous and portentous just at twilight, as the naked mountains lose completely all feeling of spatial dimension and flatten out to the quality of cardboard silhouettes on some vast stage set. One stands between two faintly defined wheel traces colored somewhat darker with volcanic pebbles than the alkali soil through which they stretch out away from you toward the horizon. And then suddenly the thought hits: "My God, this is really it! I'm standing right here on the spot where all those heretofore paper people traveled through so many long years ago in their own personal searches for something other or better than what they had left behind them."

And suddenly they are not just so many words on paper, and the horizon is no longer cardboard. Those people come alive; the whole thing ceases to be an abstraction, a mere exercise in pedantry. That particular horizon out there might not be *your* horizon, but it was as real and challenging as any you will ever set out for, and to the emigrants it was an imperative thing. They had to make it. They had no automobile parked just over the sand dune in which to speed effortlessly over concrete highways through the blistering heat of the God-forsaken barrenness. They had no motels to stop off at if suddenly fatigued or if the weather should suddenly turn too cold and threatening to sleep in the open. They had no restaurants and no supermarkets to assuage the pangs of hunger or refill the depleted larder. Here they were—just here, where you now stand—with no water for miles and miles and stock so weak that it was highly questionable whether they could make it to that river that someone or some rumor *said* was truly out there somewhere ahead.

To go on was an act of faith—faith in the word of their fellow man, faith impelled by necessity. But it was also a faith fully supported by self-reliance and determination. So they took that next step, and another, and another. They held to their faith even while pondering the awful question from which there could be no escape: if the stock did not make it to water this time, what would be their own chances of making it? Each day that was becoming a question of ever slimmer and slimmer margins. It was a matter of prevail or die. The truly remarkable thing is that along the California Trail so few did die and so many did prevail.

You stand there in their tracks now, alone in almost painfully silent wastes, and if you have any sort of feeling at all for the human species, you can't help feeling awed by the experience—awed, and humble, and proud. Those feeble but tenacious traces through the alkali dust at your feet are still there before you after more than a hundred and twenty-five years of winds and storms and unrenewal. They not only lead out of the past, but they stretch out into the future. Your feet renew them. You are there because they *were* there; it is as simple and grand as that. And in the pebble-paved continuity there is a beauty all its own, which words can never hope to approximate.

# INTRODUCTION TO THE CALIFORNIA TRAIL

## THE EMIGRANTS

"Yesterday afternoon and this morning Fremont set up his daguerreotype to photograph the rocks; he spoiled five plates that way. Not a thing was to be seen on them. That's the way it often is with these Americans. They know everything, they can do everything, and when they are put to a test, fail miserably."

Thus, in 1842, did the capable, if somewhat dour, Charles Preuss, chief cartographer to the young pathfinder John Frémont, express his candid appraisal of one facet of the American temperament. It was not completely without personal bias, and it was served up with the usual liberal portion of teutonic spleen, but it was an observation not without some merit. There was a definite measure of bluff, bravado, and impatient know-everythingness in the American then, as there is now. Preuss could see that much clearly but he couldn't see that those very qualities were to help the Americans succeed brilliantly.

Some four years later, in 1846, that intrepid mountain man, traveler, and frontier diarist extraordinaire, James Clyman, also took up the question of what made the American really tick—in this case some emigrants he had met on the way to the Pacific—and rendered this somewhat plaintive and resigned assessment:

"It is remarkable how anxious thes people are to hear from the Pacific country and strange that so many of all kinds and classes of People should sell out comfortable homes in Missouri and Elsewhere pack up and start across such an emmence Barren waste to settle some new Place of which they have at most so uncertain information but this is the character of my countrymen."

And Clyman should know; what he was skeptical about in others, he had spent most of his life doing himself! He was a traveler, a mover, a frontier American. Both he and Preuss are valuable contemporary sources for this period of American history as it relates to the great westward movement, but in the end, it is Clyman who proves to have his finger more surely on the pulse of his fellow countrymen.

For it was not so much, as Preuss's words of pique would suggest, that the typical American of his day "knew everything" and could "do everything," but rather that he knew just *enough* to be tantalized by all that great, mysterious void out there to the west beyond the horizon, known only as the Great American Desert. These people knew just enough and they could *do* just enough to make them confident that whatever was out there, they could handle it. It was precisely that other great undefined territory, that interior region that stretched from the "everything" of Preuss's thinking to the "enough" of the American pioneer, that was to be the challenge and proving ground of the westward-bound emigrant. The decade of the 1840s was to find them pushing boldly into both unknowns with some of that conceit and gall which so offended Preuss. But history was to prove Preuss quite wrong about one thing—the emigrant was not to fail miserably in what he set out to do.

But simply to state this sort of facile observation from the safety of historical hindsight is not really to explain the why of the emigrant psyche. There has to be much more to it than that, and if it puzzles us now, so, obviously, did it continue to puzzle Clyman then, for he comes back to the topic only a few weeks later. He had come upon the gravestone of a seventy-year-old emigrant, Mrs. Sarah Keyes, and the sight moved him to some philosophical speculations as to what motivates these people:

"This stone shews us that all ages and all sects are found to undertake this long tedious and even dangerous Journy for some unknown object never to be realized even by those the most fortunate and why because the human mind can never be satisfied never at rest allways on the strech for something new some strange novelty."

Clyman was still a little dubious about the prospect for success for these westward ho-ing people—after all, he had just covered the route on an eastward course, and he knew the troubles that lay out there ahead of the wagon trains—but his insight was clear and incisive. He had voiced one of the main traits of the emigrant temperament: "the strech for something new." It was a "strech" surely not unique to Americans, then or now. It was, and is, a human trait, but certainly a trait that no other nation or people in history had the freedom and opportunity to humor as the American people did. The "strech" is still an integral part of our national psyche today; only the direction of that "strech" and the perimeters of what can be considered new have been changed by the physical filling out of the continent.

But in those middle decades of the nineteenth century, America was not filled out. The nation was like a great, gangly adolescent boy, teetering on one foot on the bank of the Mississippi and destined by fatiguing muscles to lose his precarious balance at any moment and come crashing down westward. And there were plenty of both reasons and persons ready to give a little helping shove if the big splash seemed to be a little too long in coming.

The mood for expansion was everywhere, and most people saw no need for boundaries or thoughts of boundaries. The land and its treasures were there for the taking, just as their fathers had taken, and their fathers in their turn. Everyone knew that political boundaries were just set up to be broken—that was borne out by most of the history of the young republic. And yet things were a little different in the 1840s; it was no longer just a matter of political boundaries. A physical barrier now had to be considered and accommodations made for it.

The western frontier, which from the very first days of the nation had been first and always an adjunct of the vast system of interior waterways, had now reached that greatest of all riverine boundaries, the Mississippi, and its mighty tributaries. That was no particular problem—just another bigger river to cross on the western drift—but what was beyond was quite another matter. It was simply blank on most of the maps, while on some of the newer ones the words "Great American Desert" were printed across the featureless void.

Only a few mountain men and trappers and a handful of adventurers had ever been out there, and what information they did bring back was minimal, confusing, and largely unreliable. What was needed was only a convenient river or two to make travel and communication possible. A river would make that unknown barrier only another paper boundary, and everyone understood that Americans feasted on paper boundaries like grizzlies on wild berries! But were there friendly rivers out there? Some said yes and some said no, but mostly they said no.

Oh yes, there was the Platte, but it was known to be so shallow that a spider could wade across two full miles of it and never even get its stomach wet. There was no dependable route for boats and commerce up its muddy course, not even during the spring freshets. That much was pretty well known; the rest was all rumor. And such rumors! It was a land of great, towering mountains perpetually mantled in snows; it was a trackless waste of burning sands, a wilderness of tortured canyons without any vegetation, a region devoid of God's grace and hostile with incredible creatures and fierce savages. And there were stories of vast interior seas, saltier than the ocean itself, and of a great river called the Buenaventura, which flowed out of this fabulous upheaval of natural curiosities all the way to the far Pacific. Now *there* was a possibility—a river to follow, a rumor to dream on. Men should go to see if it was really there.

In the meantime, there were other things of lesser interest but more immediate concern to be considered. First of all, there were the Indians— those wild, romantic warriors of the plains, those noble aborigines, those consummate horsemen, those fierce masters of the buffalo, those savages, those heathen, those nations holding treaties with the government of the United States. *Paper* treaties! Paper treaties, paper boundaries—what's the difference? Paper is good to write on or to wad up for gun use, but not much of a thing for stopping a nation on the move. What matter if they have paper treaties; they had them before and that didn't stop us. They'll just have to let us through or move out of the way. There's plenty of land; we can't ever, not in a hundred generations, take it all. They can just move aside; we won't bother them if they don't bother us.

As for the other consideration, that was serious or not serious depending on how one reckoned it. It was true that legally most of those lands out there beyond the Mississippi did not belong to the United States. Mexico and England owned, or at least claimed, them. But really, when one thinks about it carefully, how can they claim something they can't or don't control? A paper right, you say? Enough about paper! We know what the decision is on that score well enough by now. As for the English in Oregon, they have no call on our love or respect—not with a second bloody war with them still fresh in memory. And besides, we have as much paper right to it as they have. We'll face them down on it if we can, and if we can't bluff it through—well, we walloped them twice before. In the meantime it's first come, first served, and we're a lot closer to Columbia's green shores than they are. As for Mexico, who's kidding whom? They took it all from Spain, didn't they? Why, they can't even control things at home, let alone all those millions of empty miles to the north and west. No, there isn't much of a problem there; the Mexicans are welcome to what they can keep. It may well be more legitimately theirs—but legitimately does not mean necessarily.

No, politics was the least of it. And whatever was dangerous and forbidding and unknown in between, that could be faced and overcome, too, —*provided* there was a proven way to reach the Pacific overland. And by the beginning of the 1840s a way *was* known. Trappers and missionaries and a handful of other pioneering types had already traveled a difficult but feasible route to Oregon. It was true that it was not a wagon route yet, but a way was known to be open in that direction. The remaining question was: Can a wagon make it? By the early 1840s, Americans were ready to give it a try.

It should be noted that these would-be emigrants knew that California was accessible by ship or by dangerous passage along the Santa Fe and Old Spanish trails through Mexican territory into southern California. But that was just the trouble: these westward-yearning pioneers were farmers, not seafarers; these were freeborn Americans, not quite willing to accept the whims and dictates of a foreign government; these were people who dreamed of the lush, green farmlands of central California, not the dust and sun and adobe of a southern desert clime. No, they wanted to go directly west under their own power and authority, and in a way they could afford. There was indisputably a trail to Oregon, wasn't there? Well, everyone knew Oregon was just above California, so wasn't it just possible that one could follow out that already known trail to a certain point and then strike off to California through lands that nobody really controlled?

In 1841, the Bartleson-Bidwell Party answered this proposition by doing just that. They followed the Oregon route as far as Sheep Rock, above Soda Springs in Idaho, and then struck off down the Bear River in the direction of California. In 1842, the first wagon train to Oregon, organized by Dr. Elijah White, rolled beyond Soda Springs to Fort Hall and on down the Snake River. The next year, 1843, saw Joe Walker lead his contingent of the Chiles wagon train away from the Snake River Route and establish the basic Raft River Approach to the Humboldt. A way for wagons was being pieced together bit by bit. Once a way was there; there was a market and a ready will.

There was also plenty of controversy. After all, the frontier was a place of many rumors, and rumors quickly led to debate and controversy. It was only prudent that one wonder about tales heard but not experienced personally. There always had to be a full measure of skepticism on the frontier or one didn't survive and prosper (and the desire to prosper, each in his own way, was probably the one thing that all the California-minded had in common). It paid to be suspicious and to ask sharp questions. There was just a little too much freedom and space out there along the Ohio, the Sangamon, and the Mississippi for one to act otherwise. A man could make promises, lie, work his will on you, and then disappear into endless miles of empty space, never to be heard of again. That kind of freedom made one careful, and when people did come together to talk about this chimerical place called California, there were always plenty enough to sneer and question and ridicule. As Edwin Bryant reports on one such meeting:

"The merits of the countries bordering the Pacific were discussed: by some they were denounced as abodes suitable only for the condemned and abandoned of God and man; by others they were extolled as being scarcely inferior in their attractions to the Eden described in the history of the creation, and presenting such fascination as almost to call the angels and saints from their blissful gardens and diamond temples in the heavens. Such are the antipodes of opinion among those who rely upon second-hand testimony for their information, or are governed by their prejudice, in reference to this subject."

But even sneers and ridicule couldn't stop the fever once it hit. The topic just couldn't be put to rest by the skeptics. There was always some letter from one of the few who had gone by sea to California, who was writing to his friends to come out and join him. Or there was an old trapper or mountain man who would drop by the local newspaper to affirm that all those tales were indeed true—California was the land of milk and honey. Then someone would write in to say the whole thing was a hoax and a lie, and controversy would rage again. For one who had even the least interest in the matter, there was always something to keep one's curiosity and imagination alive.

Not the least of these titillations were all those marvelous stories about the healthful climate out there in magical California. John Bidwell (who was to be in the first wagon train to California in 1841) recalls something of a meeting of prospective emigrants at which John Roubideaux, one of the first chamber-of-commerce types to pass along the virtues of the Golden State, was present and selling hard:

"Generally the first question which a Missourian asked about a country was whether there was any fever and ague. I remember his answer distinctly. He said there was but one man in California that has ever had a chill there, and it was a matter of so much wonderment to the people of Monterey that they went eighteen miles into the country to see him shake. Nothing could have been more satisfactory on the score of health. He said that the Spanish authorities were most friendly, and that the people were the most hospitable on the globe; that you could travel all over California and it would cost you nothing for horses or food. Even the Indians were friendly. His description of the country made it seem like a Paradise."

Well, if it were Paradise in 1840, by 1846 this sort of apocryphal story had been developed to the point well beyond heavenly appellations. Edwin Bryant relates for us a classic contemporary story which must surely bring color even to the cheeks of the native Californian weaned on three-hundred-and-sixty-five-days-a-year-sunshine and other such hyperbole:

"A story was told in regard to the climate of California, which, because it serves to illustrate the extravagances above referred to, I will endeavor to recite. It was of a man who had lived in California, until he had reached the advanced age of two hundred and fifty years! Although that number of years had passed over him, such were the life-giving and youth-preserving qualities of the climate, that he was in the perfect enjoyment of his health, and every faculty of mind and body which he had ever possessed. But he was tired of life. Having lived so long in a turbulent and unquiet world, he anxiously desired some new state of existence, unincumbered with its cares, and unruffled by its passions and its strifes. But not with-standing all his efforts to produce a result which he so much wished, and for which he daily and hourly prayed to his Maker, health, and vigor and life still clung to him—he could not shake them off. He sometimes con-templated suicide; but the holy *padres*, to whom he confessed his thoughts, admonished him that that was damnation: he was a devout Christian, and would not disobey their injunctions. A lay friend, however, (his *heir*, prob-ably) with whom he daily consulted on this subject, at last advised him to a course which, he thought, would produce the desired result. It was to make his will, and other arrangements, and then travel to a foreign coun-try. This suggestion was pleasing to our venerable Californian patriarch in search of death, and he immediately adopted it. He visited an adjoining country; and very soon, in accordance with his plan and his wishes, he took sick and died. In his will, however, he required his heir and executor, upon pain of disinheritance, to transport his remains to his own country and there entomb them. This requisition was faithfully complied with. His body was interred with great pomp and ceremony in his own ceme-tery, and prayers were rehearsed in all the churches for the rest of his soul. He was happy, it was supposed, in heaven, where, for a long series of years, he had prayed to be; and his heir was happy that he was there. But what a disappointment! Being brought back and interred in California soil, with the health-breathing Californian zephyrs rustling over his grave, the energies of life were immediately restored to his inanimate corpse! Hercu-lean strength was imparted to his frame, and bursting the prison walls of death, he appeared before his chapfallen heir reinvested with all the vigor and beauty of early manhood! He submitted to his fate, and determined to live his appointed time. Stories similar to the foregoing, although ab-surd and so intended, no doubt leave their impressions upon many minds predisposed to rove in search of adventures and Eldorados."

It is easy for us to smile indulgently at these outrageous tales. The emi-grants did, too—at least some of them—as Bryant's closing words indi-cate, but their laughter was tempered with an unspoken longing and a wistful hope. For in the early years before the rush for gold brought other sorts of motives, consideration of climate and health was often the decid-ing factor for many an emigrant family when that fateful time came to say a final yes or no to the proposition to pack up and go to California.

There was not a family on the frontier who hadn't in some way suffered from the debilitating effects of the ague (malaria) or felt the breath of panic when the news came that the periodic scourge of cholera or typhus was again upon the land. It is hard for us today to imagine the primitive state of the medical profession such a short time ago, but if one was sick, it was almost invariably a matter of opiates, amputation, or prayer—with the last usually the most effective. That was it. Nothing at all was known or understood about these pestilential things except that they came, and that they often—too often—came with death. And such ignorance as to the causes and nature of these diseases could only bring fear and the desire to flee that fear. No one, whatever his station might be, was immune. One might escape, but then, one also might not, and the chances were that sooner or later one would not. So these stories of a climate so perfect that the very sight of a man shaking was a cause for incredulity might indeed be laughable, but how wonderful it would be if it were true!

Many a wife must have looked over at her husband pouring over the latest newspaper for bits and scraps of news about California and then over at her sleeping children and have silently asked herself: "Could there possibly be such a place? Could we save the children and ourselves from sickness?" And quite often it was that unspoken question that found its answer the next spring in the squeaky voice of wheels rolling toward California.

There were, of course, a multitude of other reasons that motivated the emigrants for their journey west to the land of promise. For some Roman Catholics there was the added enticement of a land in which their own faith was the established church, and there was the possibility of a good, solid religious education for their children at the missions. For others, it was escape—escape from debts or too many obligations, escape from tedium, escape from a life gone slowly sour, and occasionally, escape from lawfulness. Some just had to move on; some wanted freedom, movement, adventure. Change and betterment—that was the common theme. And one suspects that not too uncommonly there just wasn't anything better to do than see what it was all about out there.

Reuben Shaw, writing in 1849, gives his assessment of emigrant motivation as follows:

"The mystery attached to the country which we were to traverse, the novelty of the undertaking, the prospect of lively adventure and, in some cases, the benefits that were expected to be derived from a change from the counting-room to life in the open air seemed to be the primary incentives to their crossing the plains."

(One should point out that by 1849, as Shaw's own journey testifies, there was that other most compelling reason of all: gold, with the promise of instant fortune. But Mr. Shaw, while alluding to the unhealthy aspect of the counting rooms at home, delicately avoids sullying his list of honorable incentives with anything as crass as honest human greed.)

In sum, there were just as many combinations of reasons as there were people and temperaments involved. And it is to those people that we must now turn our attention.

Just who were these emigrants? Again, the answer is almost a cliche: they were everyman. They were the prosperous and the poor, the intelligent and the stupid, the educated and the ignorant. They were the religious, the proper, the solid-citizen farmer and merchant. They were the sacrilegious, the lawless, the feckless youth. As a whole, particularly in the years before 1849 (before the promise of gold attracted a much less select spectrum of citizens), they were probably a superior cross section of frontier American society. In the early years and again after the gold fever subsided, they were basically family units and they were substantial

"*Little Mountain Pass*" (*later named Forty-nine Pass*), *east of Surprise Valley, California.*

enough to put together the outlay of money such a journey required. They were farmers, merchants, and professional men who saw the opportunity to be in on the start of something new. Unlike the argonauts of forty-nine and after, a sizable majority of whom were merely intent on quick riches and then a return to a comfortable life of esteem and respectability back in the States, these people were going west with the idea of sticking with it and building a new life for themselves and their children. They had cut their roots, but they were carrying along the seeds and carefully wrapped grafts of their American traditions to plant and nurture on soil they heard to be rich and deep and ripe for planting.

Francis Parkman, that sophisticated scion of the eastern establishment and recent graduate of Harvard College, on his way to do scholarly research on the American Indian, saw some of these emigrants on the trail in 1846 and generously allowed that "they were fine-looking fellows, with an air of frankness, generosity, and even courtesy, having come from one of the least barbarous of the frontier counties."

Parkman was not one to be enslaved by first impressions, however, and a little further on he updates his opinion with some show of Brahmin contempt: "Yet, for the most part, they were the rudest and most ignorant of the frontier population; they knew absolutely nothing of the country and its inhabitants; they had already experienced much misfortune, and apprehended more; they had seen nothing of mankind, and had never put their own resources to the test." A rather thorough indictment, one might think, but Parkman can be more acerbic than that, as his very first impression of the emigrants testifies:

". . . Among them are some of the vilest outcasts in the country. I have often perplexed myself to divine the various motives that give impulse to this migration; but whatever they may be, whether an insane hope of a better condition in life, or a desire of shaking off restraints of law and society, or mere restlessness, certain it is that multitudes bitterly repent the journey, and after they have reached the land of promise are happy enough to escape from it."

Well, one must grant the gentleman his opinions, but one must also regret that he was not as interested in the emigrants as he was in the Indians. He could have used his disciplined mind and fine intellect to give us valuable insight into one of the great movements of his time. He was undoubtedly right that some (certainly not "multitudes") repented bitterly their decision to make haste to the promised land—we have the written words of some who did—but there was so much more to be known about the person inside the emigrant than that.

There was another young man named Elisha Perkins, who in 1849 could sit down at the outset of his journey and face up to his own self-doubts while voicing the faith that sustained him:

"If the thousands who have gone should find themselves in the mountains without provender or caught in the snow storm what would become of them & us? We could not find sustenance sufficient for all at any of the stations on the road or at the Mormon settlements & our stock of provisions could not last us back to the U.S. & I dont see how great loss of life could be avoided. I cannot keep clear of the blues sometimes when I look at the possible result of this Expedition & think that I may have seen my last of those dear ones at home & enjoy my journey much less than if I was relieved of all uncertainty as to its termination. But I must away with such gloomy anticipations & trust to Providence to take care of me & restore me alive & well to the home I have left."

It was this same young man who could be brutally honest with himself and throw off that shell of hypocrisy which so many of his contemporary fortune seekers hid behind:

"Now we were out of civilization & the influences of civilized society entirely, & cut loose from the rest of the world to take care of ourselves for a while. I confess to a feeling of lonliness as I thought on the prospects before us, & all we were separating ourselves from behind. Henceforth we shall have no society, no sympathy in our troubles, & none of the comforts to which we have been accustomed, but must work across these vast wild wastes alone & go in our own strength & his who takes care of us all. So be it. Gold must be had & I for one am willing to brave most anything in its acqusition."

So be it, indeed. Perkins did "brave most anything" and was one of those who found not fortune but an early death in California. He died in 1852 in his early twenties.

There was also a strong woman named Jane Gould, who, in the shadow of the sinister-looking Humboldt Mountains, would finally allow herself to pour out a long pent-up and very human longing—a longing silently churning in many other hearts: "Oh dear, I do so want to get there, it is now almost four months since we have slept in a house. If I could only be set down at home with all the folks I think there would be some talking as well as resting."

And there was another pioneer woman, Lodisa Frizzell, who also thought of a house as a symbolic place to flee with her thoughts of human frailty and mortality:

"We are hardly halfway. I felt tired & weary. O the luxury of a house, a house! I felt what some one expressed who had traveled this long & tidious journey, that, 'it tries the soul.' I would have given all my interest in California, to have been seated around my own fireside surrounded by friend and relation. That this journey is tiresome, no one will doubt, that it is perilous, the deaths of many testify, and the heart has a thousand misgivings & the mind is tortured with anxiety, & often as I passed the fresh made graves, I have glanced at the side boards of the wagon, not knowing how soon it might serve as a coffin for some one of us; but thanks for the Kind care of Providence we were favored more than some others." There is the simple eloquence of real humanity here.

But it was not always a matter of solemn thoughts or pensive reveries. There could also be laughter and song and dance. There were times to get drunk, times to swear and to fight; times to sober up, and times to pray that if the good Lord were willing to let the head and stomach come back to normal, then there would be no more of that rot-gut corn likker. There were times to court and to make love. There were times to luxuriate in cool waters after a long, dusty day of travel. And there was always the saving grace of humor—the facility to step back and have a good laugh at the absurdity of this little part of the human predicament. These emigrants were capable of such humor and of inflicting upon us and themselves that atrocious genre of poetry which was both *de regle* and *de rigueur*:

> "How do you like it overland?"
> His mother she will say;
> "All right, excepting cooking,
> Then the devil is to pay.
> For some won't cook and other can't,
> And then it's curse and damn,
> The coffeepot's begun to leak
> And so's the frying-pan.

"It's always jaw about the teams,
And how we ought to do;
All hands get mad and each one says;
'I own as much as you.'
One of them says, 'I'll buy or sell,
I care not what may come';
Another says, 'Let's buy him out,
The lousy son-of-a-gun.'

"I'd rather ride a raft at sea,
Wish I'd gone around the Horn,
Than try to cook with buffalo wood—
Take some that's newly born.
The desert's nearly death on corns
While walking in the sand,
And drive a jackass by the tail—
God damn this overland."
                              —in *Hulbert*

They could also use their rhymes to be more philosophical:

Upon Pacific's distant shores is heard a startling
     cry,
A sound that wakes the nations up as swift the
     tidings fly;
An El Dorado of untold wealth—a land whose soil
     is gold,
Full many a glittering dream of wealth to mortal
     eyes unfold.

Oh gold! how mighty is thy sway, how potent is
     thy rod!
Decrepid age & tender youth acknowledge thee a God;
At thy command the world is sway'd, as on the deep
     blue sea,
The Storm King rules the elements that roll so
     restlessly.
And see, the crowd is rushing now across the arid
     plain,
All urged by different passions on, yet most by
     thirst of gain;

And I, my home & native state, have left thy genial
    shade,
To throw my banner to the breeze where wealth,
    like dreams, is made.

—in *Geiger*

The emigrants could, indeed, smile and versify, but there were times
when the days were just too long and hot, the dust too stifling, the ever-
building pressures too much. Then was the time to let it all out with a very
human snarl, as James Wilkins was constrained to do at Gravelly Ford on
the Humboldt:

"Early this morn^g we started, and found the country as baren as it is
possible to conceive.  piles of huge hills covered with sage brush, nothing
else which ever way the eye turned, accompanied with the usual portion of
dust.  speaking of dust, it is found to be one of the most annoying evils of
the route.  towards evening, arriving at the river, found every particle of
grass eat off.  there never had been much, but every blade was gone. We
hunted down the River 3 miles more, and found but a very scanty picking
for the oxen.  every body hungry and out of humour as usual.  with difficulty quarrels are avoided. From what I can hear, and I speak to almost
every company I see, I don't think there ever was a body of men left the
state, on any expedition, that had so much quarrelling and fighting, (the
strong abusing the weak,) as the California expedition in 1849."

There was plenty of this orneriness, petty meanness, anger, quarreling,
and even at times brutality recorded among the emigrants. They were not
angels, these searchers for paradise; they were mere mortals put through a
dreadful physical and mental ordeal.

And if you think that after the ordeal was over—the dust and thirst and
hunger, the deserts and mountains, the doubts and fears and anguish all
left behind—they all liked what they found at the end of the rainbow,
well, you aren't granting them their true measure of humanity. Elisha
Perkins took one quick look at this hard-won Garden of Eden along the
Sacramento and fairly roared forth his disillusionment:

"Never was there such misrepresentation as about this country, both
as to the futility, fertility or capability of cultivation, & richness of the
mines, & all that a few men might make fortunes. Among the Emigrants
you will hear Bryant, Frémont, Robinson & others whose published ac-
counts were the chief inducement to many to leave their comfortable

Here to forks – Cherokee Guide
Forks to gap or pass in mountains –   12
springs ½ m. to left of road)
Thence to Rabbit Hole Springs ———   13
" " Black Rock &c ———   20
(7 m. beyond B.R. boil'g Sp's. plenty.)
" " Mud Lake ————   20

About 5 m. S. of R. Hole Springs are
hot Spr'gs, & grass plains. If the road
could go that way it would be
longer, but probably better.

" " Last Hot Spring ———   3
" " Salt Valley ————   20
" " 1st Camp in Hight Rock Cañon   10
Up H. R. Cañon ————   20
Thence to Little Mountain Pass –   18
6 m. from the last water of high rock
creek to a good camp at a running
brook; 2 m. more, on left of road,
are Springs: Grass & water both sides
of pass.
Thence to Warm Springs ———   12
Summit of Sierra Nevada
Plenty of grass & water all

168

*Jesse Applegate's waybill, from Bruff's copy of the "Cherokee Guide" to Lassen's Route.*

homes, cussed up & down, & loaded with all kinds of opprobrious names. They have all amassed fortunes off of the Emigration they have induced. This valley presents few attraction to any one who has lived in the states. No beautiful forests, or rich meadows but very few singing birds, *Except Owls*, & these abound. There are some Elk in the plains & any quantity of wolves, also in the sloughs great numbers of cranes, geese, duck &c, but every one without exception is disappointed both in the appearance of the country & the richness of vegetable or mineral productions."

Those dry, shriveled-up plains, those blistering hot, seared-over, brown foothills, those dirty, squalid, ragtag mining camps, those blocks of tents which passed for cities just didn't seem to square with the sort of picture conjured up by a man such as Lansford W. Hastings in his *Emigrant's Guide to Oregon and California:*

"In view of their increasing population, accumulating wealth, and growing prosperity, I can not but believe, that the time is not distant, when those wild forests, trackless plains, untrodden valleys, and the un-bounded ocean, will present one grand scene, of continuous improve-ments, universal enterprise, and unparalleled commerce: when those vast forests, shall have disappeared, before the hardy pioneer; those extensive plains, shall abound with innumerable herds, of domestic animals; those fertile valleys shall groan under the immense weight of their abundant products: when those numerous rivers, shall team with countless steam-boats, steam-ships, ships, barques and brigs; when the entire country, will be everywhere intersected, with turnpike roads, railroads and canals; and when, all the vastly numerous, and rich resources, of that now, almost un-known region, will be fully and advantageously developed."

Words of prophecy, when read today, but how ironic and bitter they or others like them must have seemed to a bewildered, resentful young man as he stood in the midst of this prophecy only four years after it was pub-lished and felt used and betrayed.

And yet, how resilient youth is! After a good night's sleep and a decent meal or two, without the awful pressure of the journey, Perkins could re-gain his perspective and good humor, and concede:

"On a review of our journey & its incidents now that it is all over & our sufferings & privations at an end, I would not have it differ in any respect from what it was, we saw everything of frontier travelling that could be seen & struck the life in all its varieties, with wagon, packs & on foot, & the harder the times we had the pleasanter the retrospect, by contrast.

Dearly have I paid for my experience to be sure, both pecuniarily &
physically, but I should know now exactly how to go back by the same
route both pleasantly & speedily, & at much less expense, & consider myself pretty well qualified to give advice to any of my friends who wish to
try the same journey."


Yes, the thing was done, and much had been learned by trial and tribu-
lation. Perkins can be excused the pride which shows through his words.
He had been one of the many who had successfully taken part in one of the
great feats of American history. It took a lot to do it—determination, perseverance, faith, lots of brutally hard work, a little luck now and then, and
one other thing that should be fully recognized: the adaptability of the
human animal.

Franklin Langworthy takes up this theme toward the end of his journey
in 1850 and embellishes it with a little local color and slightly lugubrious
detail:

"'A man may get used to anything,' is an old saying, the truth of which
is pretty clearly demonstrated on this journey. Traveling in constant
clouds of dust, dirty faces, hands, and clothes, become less and less offen-
sive, so that as we draw towards the termination of the journey, we see for
a general rule, a dirty rabble. Men have stomachs that are far from being
squeamish. I have seen a man eating his lunch, and gravely sitting upon
the carcass of a dead horse, and we frequently take our meals amidst the
effluvia of a hundred putrescent carcases. Water is drank with a good relish, into which we know that scores of dead animals have been thrown, or
have fallen. I saw three men eating a snake the other day, that one of them
had dressed and cooked, not because they were in want of food, but as a
rarity, or perhaps, rather by way of bravo, to show others that nothing
would turn their stomachs. Graves of emigrants are numerous on this side
of the Desert. The usual mode of burying the dead on this route, is to dig
a very shallow grave, inter the corpse without coffin, and set up a narrow
piece of board by way of monument, on which a brief inscription is cut
with a knife. Many, however, have only a split stick set up, into which a
paper is put, on which the inscription is written."

For some did die. They died and were consigned to the sands of the des-

*Grave markers, scattered like milestones along the trail, gave testimony to its hazards.*

erts or the shallow sod of alpine meadows. There was no end of places to slip a fallen comrade or a loved one. The desert took, the mountain took, the river took. But probably they took not much more than would have been taken back home. After all, those were taking times, no matter where one was.

The hardest thing was to leave someone behind that way, shallow in the soil and with only a flimsy wooden plank to do the remembering. It wasn't right, but the trail was just too long to be a properly tended cemetery. The markers would fall before the winds and not be set up again; the coyotes and birds and ants would do the rest. Everyone knew that it wasn't right or proper, but it was needful, and what was needful man could steel his heart and do. William Warner said it for them all when he said, "Who would have thought that I could have endured such a journey besides standing guard every third night and sometimes I have stood guard four successive nights—but of all animals that cross the plains man is the toughest and can endure the most."

And endure they did. For every one left behind along the trail, hundreds came on, and a continent was spanned and a nation filled out. And many of those people reached the shores of the Pacific, or the fields of Monterey or Sonoma or Santa Clara, or the boisterous gold fields of Hangtown or Coloma or Sonora carrying a well-thumbed little book called Ware's *Emigrants' Guide to California*, a guide which closed with this parting exhortation:

"A word before we part, you are now in a country different from that which you left. Recollect that you are a component part of the country. Oppose all violations of order, and just law.—Unite with the well disposed to sustain the rights of individuals whenever incroached upon. Introduce at the earliest practical moment, those institutions which have conspired to raise our beloved country to the highest elevation of Nations:—Let schools, churches, beneficial societies, courts, &c., be established forthwith. Make provision for the forth coming millions that shortly shall people your ample valleys, and golden hills—and above all, recollect that *'righteousness exalteth a nation.'*"

We don't cotton to that kind of language much any more. These are sophisticated times. Such rhetoric is a little too old-fashioned, too pompous, too moralistic, too stilted for our ears. Values change; things move on; much is lost. Perhaps the loss is ours.


# ᴄһᴇ ɪɴᴅɪᴀɴꜱ

"We had now entered a country inhabited by these people; and as in the course of our voyage we shall frequently meet with them in various stages of existence, it will be well to remark that, scattered over the great region west of the Rocky Mountains and south of the Great Snake River, are numerous Indians whose subsistence is almost solely derived from roots and seeds, and such small animals as chance and great good fortune sometimes bring within their reach. They are miserably poor, armed only with bows and arrows, or clubs; and as the country they inhabit is almost destitute of game, they have no means of obtaining better arms. In the northern part of the region just mentioned they live generally in solitary families; and farther to the south they are gathered together in villages.

"Those who live together in villages, strengthened by association, are in exclusive possession of the more genial and richer parts of the country, while the others are driven to the ruder mountains and to the more inhospitable parts of the country. . . .

"Roots, seeds, and grass, every vegetable that affords any nourishment, and every living animal thing, insect or worm, they eat. Nearly approaching to the lower animal creation, their sole employment is to obtain food; and they are constantly occupied in a struggle to support existence" (Frémont, 1843).

No consideration of the California Trail would be complete without attention being paid to the indigenous people the emigrants encountered on this section of their great trek westward. These various Indian tribes were lumped together under the catch-all term "Diggers," and almost without exception the emigrant writings refer to them with contempt, ridicule, and downright loathing. It is very fashionable today for sympathetic writers to take the part of the Indian in any conflict with the white intruder and to write their words with the purple ink of irony and pathos. Such an approach is, of course, entirely legitimate for the historical novel, but it is certainly not acceptable in any effort that strives to maintain a semblance of historical objectivity. Whatever one's own personal sympathies may be, it is not for us of later generations, with our own ideas of social and political equity, to damn or excuse or attempt to ameliorate these harsh judgments of the emigrants. Our only legitimate task is to give the record as it is and then, at most, attempt to explain the reasons for that record and for the trouble along the turbid waters of the Humboldt.

Before we undertake that task, however, some attention must be devoted to the pesky matter of tribal terminology. From the very first, there was considerable confusion among the whites as to just where these Indians of the California Trail fit into the general scheme of tribal relationships. Were they Shoshones, or Snakes, or Utes, or Bannocks, or Paiutes, or just what? It was a problem of some ethnological complexity, and with

*A "Digger"—the emigrants' name for all California and Nevada Indians—grinding acorns at Lassen's Rancho.*

that impatience and ingenuity that was part of their Yankee heritage, the emigrants simply eschewed the subtleties of the thing and called the whole kit and caboodle of them Diggers. It was as inaccurate as it was expedient, because the Indians along the trail, while generally sharing the same culture as impressed upon them by their harsh environment, were not all of one tribe or language group.

From the fork where the California Trail broke off from the route to Oregon at Raft River to the great sink of the Humboldt, the Indians were of the Shoshone Nation. The Goshiutes, a primitive, horseless, food-gathering tribe, were the Indians indigenous to the region from the Raft River to a point about halfway down the Humboldt. They were the poor country cousins of the Snakes and Bannocks, who ranged the Snake River country and claimed the better areas for themselves. (These last mentioned two tribes, with whom the emigrants were exposed to have occasional contact, were likely to have horses and display a style and demeanor more consistent with the culture of the Plains Indians. They were not as familiar to the emigrants as the Sioux and Cheyennes and Pawnees, but they at least knew the value of a good horse and wouldn't eat it. And they still commanded, if only by association, that measure of grudging respect born out of a range of sentiments from fear to outright admiration which the emigrant held for the tribes of the horse-and-buffalo culture.) However, from a line just east of present-day Winnemucca, Nevada, to the region of the Washo tribe, another linguistic group which inhabited the area around Lake Tahoe, Reno, and Carson City, the trail passed through lands occupied by various bands of Northern Paiutes. Thus the emigrants met successively Goshiutes, Paiutes, and Washoes, all of whom, as well as the various tribes of the California mountains and foothills, were to receive the umbrella appellation "Diggers."

The derivation of the term was two-fold. Not only did these people dig out of the ground those roots and grubs and rodents that made up a chief part of their diet, but as Zenas Leonard tells us in one of the earliest descriptions we have of these people:

"Their habitations are formed of a round hole dug in the ground, over which sticks are placed, giving it the shape of a potatoe hole—this is covered with grass & earth—the door at one side and the fire at the other. They cook in a pot made of stiff mud, which they lay upon the fire & burn; but from the sandy nature of the mud, after cooking a few times, it falls to pieces, then they make a new one." These wretched creatures not only had repulsive eating habits, they actually holed up like wild animals in the ground!

Leonard goes on to give a fuller account of their primitive existence:

"These Indians are totally naked—both male and female—with the exception of a shield of grass, which they wear around their loins. They are generally small and weak, and some of them very hairy. They subsist upon grass-seed, frogs, fish, &c.—Fish, however, are very scarce—their manner of catching which, is somewhat novel and singular. They take the leg-bone of a sandhill crane, which is generally about 18 inches long, this is fastened in the end of a pole—they then, by means of a raft made of rushes, which are very plenty—float along the surface of these lakes, and spear the fish. They exhibit great dexterity with this simple structure—sometimes killing a fish with it at a great distance. They also have a kind of hook by which they sometimes are very successful, but it does not afford them as much sport as the spear. This hook is formed of a small bone, ground down on a sand-stone, and a double beard put in it with a flint— they then have a line made of wild flax. This line is tied nearest the beard end of the hook, by pulling the line the sharp end with the beard, catches, and turns the bone crossways in its mouth.

"These lakes are all joined together by means of the river which passes from one to another, until it reaches the largest, which has no out-let. The water in this lake becomes stagnant and very disagreeable—its surface being covered with a green substance, similar to a stagnant frog pond. In warm weather there is a fly, about the size and similar to a grain of wheat, on this lake, in great numbers.—When the wind rolls the waters onto the shore, these flies are left on the beach—the female Indians then carefully gather them into baskets made of willow branches, and lay them exposed to the sun until they become perfectly dry, when they are laid away for winter provender. These flies, together with grass seed, and a few rabbits, is their principal food during the winter season." This was truly existence on its most fundamental basis.

But one must not get the idea that the term "Digger" was merely some sort of quasiscientific, clinically impersonal appellation, descriptive of the life-style of a primitive people. Its connotations were far more sinister than that, and it very soon came to be an epithet of the vilest sort in the lexicon of the emigrant, for it was these seemingly cowed and thoroughly degraded Indians who were to cause the emigrants the most unrelenting and constant trouble.

We are accustomed for a variety of reasons (not the least of which is the motion picture) to thinking of the Plains Indians—those strong-jawed, noble-statured, hard-riding, feather-flying stereotyped warriors of the plains—as being the great nemeses of the emigrant, but in the early days, this just was not the case. It was not until the bloody decades of the sixties and seventies when the Plains Indians came to realize that their hunter-horseman-buffalo culture just could not accommodate the white man's encroachments and still survive, that the eastern end of the Emigrant Trail saw Indian warfare—and of course by then it was too late for the Indian. In the forties and fifties the emigrants had little to fear at all from the tribes of the Great Plains, except for the annoyance of a little stealing, an occasional attempt at blackmail, and the obligatory "scare" of a supposed Indian attack. The real troubles came only when the wagons reached the Humboldt and this primitive, non-horse culture of the Diggers was encountered. It can easily be seen that the very subsistence nature of their society made conflict almost inevitable.

There was trouble for the white man from the very first along the banks of this strange desert river. Peter Skene Ogden, who in 1828-29 was the first to trap for beaver along what he called the Unknown River, had trouble with the Indians. He managed to escape from a serious, perhaps fatal, confrontation with them only by putting up a strong show of resistance and then making a prudent and hasty retreat. The next expedition into the region in 1833, led by Joseph Reddeford Walker and chronicled for us by the aforementioned Zenas Leonard and also by Washington Irving in his *Adventures of Captain Bonneville*, led to more serious conflict and the slaughter of a large number of Indians. Leonard narrates the incident:

"Early in the morning we resumed our journey along the lakes, without seeing any signs of the Indians until after sunrise, when we discovered them issuing from the high grass in front, rear, and on either side of us. This created great alarm among our men, at first, as we thought they had surrounded us on purpose, but it appeared that we had only *happened* amongst them, and they were as much frightened as us. From this we turned our course from the border of the lake into the plain. We had not travelled far until the Indians began to move after us—first in small numbers, but presently in large companies.—They did not approach near until we had travelled in this way for several hours, when they began to send small parties in advance, who would solicit us most earnestly to stop and smoke with them. After they had repeated this several times, we began to understand their motive—which was to detain us in order to let their whole force come up and surround us, or to get into close quarters with us, when their bows and arrows would be as fatal and more effective then [*sic*] our firearms. We now began to be a little stern with them, and gave them to understand, that if they continued to trouble us, they would do it at their own risk. In this manner we were teased until a party of 80 or 100 came forward, who appeared more saucy and bold than any others. This greatly excited Capt. Walker, who was naturally of a very cool temperament, and he gave orders for the charge, saying that there was nothing equal to a good start in such a case. This was sufficient. A number of our men had never been engaged in any fighting with the Indians, and were anxious to try their skill. When our commander gave his consent to chastise these Indians, and give them an idea of our strength, 32 of us dismounted and prepared ourselves to give a severe blow. We tied our extra horses to some shrubs and left them with the main body of our company, and then selected each a choice steed, mounted and surrounded this party of Indians. We closed in on them and fired, leaving thirty-nine dead on the field—which was nearly the half—the remainder were overwhelmed with dismay—running into the high grass in every direction, howling in the most lamentable manner.

"Capt. Walker then gave orders to some of the men to take the bows of the fallen Indians and put the wounded out of misery. The severity with which we dealt with these Indians may be revolting to the heart of the philanthropist; but the circumstances of the case altogether atones for the cruelty. It must be borne in mind, that we were far removed from the hope of any succour in case we were surrounded, and that the country we were in was swarming with hostile savages, sufficiently numerous to devour us. Our object was to strike a decisive blow. This we did—even to a greater extent than we had intended."

This first battle was a tragic affair, which was to have its consequences long into the coming years and was to lead directly to the continuing hardships and sufferings of subsequent emigrant trains. The stunned Indians never forgot nor forgave what had happened to them in that fateful encounter. It was true that they seldom again joined together for a frontal attack on the white man and his rolling houses as they labored through the dust and heat of the Humboldt Valley—they held a healthy respect for the stick that spoke fire and sounded thunder! It was also true that only an occasional foolish straggler was ever actually killed in the ensuing years by the Diggers, but they made effective and terrible war on the white man's cattle and horses. Just how effective they were in this type of guerrilla warfare can perhaps best be measured in the reports of the emigrants themselves. Some of the outraged anger and contempt of the pioneer victim seethes to the surface in these remarks by Jay Green, who ran the awful gauntlet in 1852:

"This part of the journey is considered very dangerous as the traveler is obliged to pass through the root digger tribe  a nation of Indians cammence on the head waters of the Humboldt and is continued to the settlements of California  these Indians are wild and verry hostile, they lurk along the river for the purpos of stealing stock, many of them have bin killed by the mountaineers and are no more regarded by them than a

50

woolf—they are generally small in stature  ill formed and verry ugly features  many of them are covered with hair so mutch so as to have the appearance of an orang-outang. Their feet is thick and of a bean or corn shape and almost as hard as a hoof. Their weapons are the bow and arrow sharp pointed stick and sharp flints  They open the graves of the dead that are buried in their land for the purpose of stealing the garments which are buried with them."

So, they were not only cowards and thieves, they were grave-robbers and defilers of the dead! They were a scourge upon the land!

And seldom it was—very seldom—that a wagon train got through that dreadful region of rocks and willows and tall grass without serious, sometimes critical, loss of stock. To the trail-weary emigrants, this was a final burden of misfortune which could only lead to their considering the natives with outrage and contempt. These unspeakable savages not only struck at night and from ambush, but they also didn't have the guts to come out and war on human beings, who could at least fight back! No, they sneaked up and stole stock under the cover of night or shot them full of arrows so that they had to be abandoned. They didn't capture horses to ride, like any self-respecting Indian would do; they captured them *to eat*, and then they staggered off to some hole in the ground to lie with bloody faces and ugly, bloated bellies to belch themselves into satiated sleep and dream of further orgies! They were surely the absolute bottom of the barrel of humanity. They fully deserved to be shot down on sight, or tied up and whipped, or have poison larded in their ill-gotten fare to give them the just recompense of a terrible, agonized death. Fortunate indeed was the captured Digger whose humane treatment was described in the year 1849 by Isaac Wistar:

"The water gets still worse and more impregnated with mineral. Grass has nearly disappeared, being only found in small patches in the river bends, where it has to be diligently searched for by advance parties. The mules look badly, some of them showing signs of failure. While looking for grass ahead of the wagons, tonight, three of us flushed, rode down, and caught a Digger. He was short, stout and naked except for a small grass bonnet on his ugly head. He had secreted his arms, if he had any, and displayed in a split stick a small eel, doubtless reserved for a family feast. As the miserable wretch stood with lariat round his neck, rolling his longing eyes from us to the free but distant hills, it seemed hard to take his worthless and joyless life, notwithstanding his undoubted proclivity for potting men and mules in the darkness. Yet one man voted for his death, and when outvoted, insisted that he should be 'tied up and whipped a little, anyhow.' I am happy to say his philanthropic view was not allowed to prevail."

There was still some compassion to be brought up from the deep well of humanity, but not much. Those were terrible miles down the Humboldt, miles that didn't encourage much soft-heartedness. There was the conflict with the land and the conflict between cultures, and one cannot hope to adequately understand the causes of this continuing human conflict without attempting to understand the fundamental incompatibility of the beleaguered emigrants' state of mind at this crucial point in the journey and the very real need of the Digger to survive.

By the time the emigrants reached the Humboldt, they were almost always in varying degrees of serious trouble. The precise amount of that trouble depended a great deal on their own individual allotments of prudence and good luck. Most were running short of food. Wagons were in bad repair and the stock in poor shape after over a thousand miles on the trail. People were short of temper and taut of nerve. Often they were weak from sickness and from improper diet. Even at the very best, they were bone-weary of travel and desperately longing for the ordeal of the journey to be over.

Against this background state of highly volatile mental and emotional anguish, they knew that they still had hundreds of miles ahead of them across desert valleys and mountains, and along the banks of a river unlike any sort of river ever known to them before. It was a sinister, spooky river, a river that started out of the desert mountains and ended sinking away into a foul-smelling, undrinkable swamp of a sink. It was almost as though the devil himself had thought it up to add more misery to their already more than ample portion. And after that damnable river, there was the dreaded purgatory of the Forty Mile Desert to be crossed and, yet beyond that, the awesome Sierra Nevada with its precipitous eastern escarpment and those seemingly endless miles of rocky, tree-shrouded ridges and canyons! After the fateful winter of 1846, there was always in the back of every mind the knowledge of that ill-fated group that didn't make it over in time and were forced into the ultimate degradation of eating human flesh to survive.

Not only was nature evilly weighted against them, but so was time. They had to hurry; they must push on. They must beat the snows to the passes. And then, as though all this torment of pressing troubles weren't enough, those damn Diggers skulked about wounding and killing the stock upon whose health and strength to move their very lives depended. Small wonder that there was hatred and contempt for the Digger.

Few of the emigrants who went through that alkali hell would be even as charitable as James Clyman was in saying, "I will merely state that it is easy to make a savage of a civilised man but impossible to make a civilised man of a savage in one Generation." For most of the emigrants, it wasn't a question of raising the poor, cursed Diggers to even a rudimentary state of civilization; it was a question of first making them human!

Unfortunately for the Digger and his point of view, we have no contemporary written records upon which to draw to balance out this picture. Even so, it is perhaps permissible for us from this remote and uninvolved point in history to look back and offer some speculations concerning the Indian side of this confrontation of cultures, which would seem to have some measure of validity.

*A scene at Johnson's Ranch, east of Sacramento at the end of the Stevens-Donner Route.*

The first of these must be the observation that even though the bands along the Humboldt were not above the most basic food-gathering level of subsistence, they were completely and rather beautifully attuned to their environment. Indeed, in the vernacular of our times, they must be granted that much-vaunted accolade of being in complete equilibrium ecologically.

They were a people who didn't in any way disrupt or attempt to change the natural order of things; they fit themselves into the seasonal cycles and took whatever chanced to come their way. They occupied a difficult ecological niche, which was not attractive to their neighbors, and consequently they were largely protected from encroachment and human competition. Effectively, they functioned in a closed system, a system protected by both topography and their own primitiveness. They had no property or accumulation of wealth that might serve to arouse the covetousness of their neighbors. They had no agriculture or domesticated animals. They had only simple tools and primitive shelters. They were semi-nomadic gatherers and hunters who followed and exploited a seasonal food supply. They were completely at the mercy of the weather, and their social structure was primarily the single-family unit, rather loosely drawn together into bands or tribes, depending on food sources for their identities. Thus, they called themselves Cattail-Eaters or Trout-Eaters or Ground-Squirrel-Eaters within the context of the larger Paiute Nation. It was all very primitive.

And yet, despite this primitiveness—or rather *because* of it—they were able to survive in one of the harshest and least inviting environments of the continent, and they were able to survive only because they made use of absolutely everything that the desert presented to them in the way of sustenance. Anything and everything was utilized, from grubs and insects and roots to ground squirrels, rats, birds, seeds, waterfowl, grasshoppers, rabbits, and antelope. And if they did not relish it all, at least they intuited that the exigencies of survival did not allow the luxury of a discriminating palate. That was the privilege of plentitude, and theirs was a life always poised on the edge of scarcity.

Nothing in this sort of culture could ever be anything but semipermanent, because the desert environment was itself in constant flux. The Diggers could survive in one spot only so long as there was sufficient food and water to sustain life. They did gather together into bands and inhabit certain of the choicer sites—the river bottoms and the shores of interior lakes, where supplies of food were relatively constant—but rarely was there enough of a surplus to guarantee a fixed settlement.

The availability of food dictated all movements, and food depended on the caprices of nature. Let the rains be too light one year or the winter too long and cold, and they had to move on; let the piñon nut crop be marginal in one range of mountains (as was the natural run of events), and they would have to seek out another area where the crop was adequate; let the spring freshets from the Sierra emptying into desert lakes be heavy, and they could gorge themselves on spawning salmon-trout and the great black lake-suckers until their stomachs could simply swell no more; let the freshets be light, and there would be little singing and much hunger.

Indeed, the specter of famine was always before them; it was ever just behind the next cloud or gust of frigid wind, or just over the next rocky ridge where their people had once gathered cattails and tules, but where now there was only sun-scorched stubble and alkali mud stretching out in almost geometric reticulations toward the distant horizon; or the ground itself shook and roared, and waters that had forever in memory flowed ceased to flow and give life. In such a desert environment, nature is supreme above all things and all configurations of society. A man survives only by taking all there is to be had in a season and then moving on.

Into this delicately balanced equilibrium between natural production and human consumption and survival came the white man. First he came only to take the beaver and the muskrat from the river, and he quickly departed. This first assault on the marshes and rivers must have caused concern to the Indian, but it was not a thing of overwhelming trauma. After all, the beavers were few enough and not that essential to the Diggers' survival—beavers were that very slimmest of margins that could be sacrificed without throwing the whole system out of kilter. But that was all that could be sacrificed; this first intrusion fully alerted the Digger to the potential threat of the white man.

Then the next white men came. The Indians remembered and approached—perhaps with hostility, certainly with curiosity—and the white men answered them with death. Then they, too, were gone, and it was several years before others of their kind returned. First they came on foot or on horseback; they moved through quickly and caused little disruption. But then they came in greater numbers, in houses that moved across the earth like so many clouds scudding down from the mountains. They came in a season, too, just like the spawning salmon-trout, but they were not part of the natural cycle of things. They came in ever increasing numbers, and they brought herds of horses, oxen, and cattle, who ate the grass, devoured the seeds, trampled the willows, and stripped the autumn berries from the bushes. And they carried those awful sticks which could speak like thunder and kill the rabbit and duck and antelope and sage hen without all that patient tracking or use of ingenious snare, which were all part of the proper balance.

And kill they did. They took much, and what game they didn't kill, they scared away from the river valleys. From his hideaways up on the mountain sides, the Digger could look down and witness that subtle equilibrium of nature upon which his own life and that of his family depended being eaten and hoofed and shot into oblivion. Not only was the game killed or driven away, but these houses on wheels stopped in the choicest places between the mountains and the river, leaving the Indian cut off effectively from his most vital and important source of food and shelter.

It is not hard to imagine the despised Digger, witnessing in his turn this devastation of his traditional pattern of existence (an isolated existence which, except for occasional brief forays of horse-riding Utes or Snakes, had seldom before been interrupted and never then for any length of time) and saying to himself: "Well, turnabout is fair enough! These white-faces have destroyed my seeds and grasses, killed and scared off my game, cut me off from my fish and roots and water, and killed my people when we came to see why they did these things and warn them away. So be it! They have taken from us; now we will take from them. They have plenty of cattle and horses. We will kill them and take what we must have to survive. We will live well off these white-faces."

And so the need of the emigrant gave rise to the need of the Indian; one set of miseries gave rise to another, and a vicious cycle of self-perpetuating hostilities was begun. The white men disrupted the ancient pattern of this desert people and thus had to pay the full price of that disruption in terms of stealthily slaughtered livestock, livestock both groups critically needed to insure their own survival. One might be tempted to see a glimmer of poetic justice in this cycle of events, except that from the very first it was a cycle heavily weighted against the Indian. The wagon trains and their walking commissaries only moved through the region during a few months of the year and then were gone, leaving the Digger behind with his badly disrupted environment and nothing to compensate him for his losses. When the frigid winds of winter blew down from the Sierra and the emigrants were all safely down the slopes beyond into the Sacramento Valley, the Indian couldn't go out and zing an arrow into a grazing cow, nor could he slice a nice hunk of mule meat for his hungry family. Instead, a great chunk had been sliced out of the flesh of one of the most productive seasons in his own cycle of survival, and only the most desperate gathering of available foods at either end of the emigrant season would suffice to insure him against starvation and disaster.

Some sense of the turmoil and desperation and fear that must have been experienced by the Indians at this catastrophic turn of events can be gleaned from a remarkable book entitled *Life Among the Piute*, which was published in 1883 by Sarah Winnemucca Hopkins. Sarah was the granddaughter of the Paiute chief Truckee, who befriended and guided the Stevens Party in 1843 and remained a loyal friend of the white man to his death. Sarah was probably born in 1844 (she was not certain), and the reportage of these early contacts between whites and Indians is obviously hearsay, but one should not dismiss it as being historically invalid just on that account. The oral tradition is strong in non-writing cultures, and while dates and figures and chronological sequences may end up a little jumbled, the substance of the recollection may well be very accurate. At any rate, this little book by a most extraordinary woman is the closest thing to the Indian side of the encounter that we are ever going to have.

In it Sarah quotes her father (who had been named chief of all the Northern Paiutes by her grandfather before he went off to California with his white brothers) as calling all the bands of Paiutes together at the sink of the Carson one spring and telling them of some dreams that had come to him. He prefaced his remarks with these words:

"These white people must be a great nation, as they have houses that move. It is wonderful to see them move along. I fear we will suffer greatly by their coming to our country; they come for no good to us, although my father said they were our brothers, but they do not seem to think we are like them. What do you all think about it? Maybe I am wrong. My dear children, there is something telling me that I am not wrong, because I am sure they have minds like us, and think as we do; and I know that they were doing wrong when they set fire to our winter supplies. They surely knew it was our food."

Then, the dream:

"'I dreamt this same thing three nights,—the very same. I saw the greatest emigration that has yet been through our country. I looked North and South and East and West, and saw nothing but dust, and I heard a great weeping. I saw women crying, and I also saw my men shot down by the white people. They were killing my people with something that made a great noise like thunder and lightning, and I saw the blood streaming from the mouths of my men that lay all around me. I saw it as if it was real. Oh, my dear children! You may all think it is only a dream,— nevertheless, I feel that it will come to pass. And to avoid bloodshed, we must all go to the mountains during the summer, or till my father comes back from California. He will then tell us what to do. Let us keep away from the emigrant roads and stay in the mountains all summer, and we can lay up great supplies for the coming winter, and if the emigrants don't come too early, we can take a run down and fish for a month, and lay up dried fish. I know we can dry a great many in a month, and young men can go into the valleys on hunting excursions, and kill as many rabbits as they can. In that way we can live in the mountains all summer and all winter too.'"

Now it is recognized that Sarah Winnemucca's book is not to be considered as a primary source reference for these early days along the California Trail. It is a secondary source and one written in the flowery and sentimental Victorian style of the time by an Indian woman passionately crusading for the rights and dignity of her people. One must recognize the bias and perhaps be a little suspect of the prose of her father's speech— prose which reads a little too patently like one of those "noble savage" monologues out of a Western to be fully credited with authenticity.

But perhaps the real point to be made is that if her father didn't say these things, he (or someone like Sarah for him) *should* have said them. They ring absolutely true in the historical context as we know it. And they must have rung true to Sarah, who as a little child remembers being buried under the sand with her cousin for a whole day because they just couldn't run fast enough to keep up with her mother after the word came that the whites were coming to eat them all up. For her to have put them in the mouth of her father would not at all lessen their value as expressing a sentiment which had the ring of an ultimate personal truth and tragedy to it.

Certainly the old ways of the Indian, the Digger, were doomed. That serious and successful flirtation with the subtle caprices of nature was soon to be a thing of the past; that delicately established and carefully maintained equilibrium between desert gatherer and his beautiful, if harsh and begrudging, environment was already hopelessly out of balance. The scale had been tipped away from the Indian forever by the weight of that first wagon wheel.

# the land

The land through which the emigrants passed on the California Trail is geologically and scenically some of the most varied, contrasting, and interesting to be found on the North American continent.

In the western reaches it is a land completely dominated by the lofty Sierra Nevada of California, and with the exception of some few miles at the beginning, which are drained by the great Snake-Columbia river system, the entire central section through Nevada passes through the high desert country of the Great Basin. This is seismically active country, overwhelmingly volcanic in origin, with occasional mountain spines of granite. It is high country with extremes of cold and heat, and elevations generally above four thousand feet. It is dry country, with mostly sparse vegetation, and thus its geologic components are essentially naked to the eye and sharply etched. It is a land of blinding dust storms and fierce winds. It is a land of crystalline nights when the Milky Way flows ever so liquidly above and a shooting star streaks so seemingly near that one could surely reach right up and catch it if one dared. It is a land one has to understand if one would understand the dismay, the hardship, the challenge, and, occasionally, the joy and pleasure it gave to the emigrant.

The term *Great Basin* was coined by Frémont to describe that vast area of the western United States in which a system of closed, interior drainage was to be found. In this area all precipitation collects into landlocked basins rather than flowing to the oceans. Unfortunately for the sake of precision, Frémont's term is not as descriptive as it might be because it suggests that there is just *one* great basin when in reality this is a region of many basins separated by intervening ranges of mountains.

These ranges are parallel to each other and are orientated on a general north-south axis following the direction of the major fault zones. They are actually great blocks of the earth's surface that have been tilted up along one side and depressed along the other as a result of the crumpling of the

[DESCENT INTO HIGH ROCK CAÑON]

*The steep, stony approach to High Rock Canyon was one of many difficult passages for the wagons.*

earth's crust. In attempting to give a helpful and graphic representation of this sort of topography, one is tempted to have recourse to the simile of an old-fashioned washboard with its alternating ridges and troughs, but that would undoubtedly lead to the very false impression that these series of alternating valleys and mountains were all of uniform length and equal size. To get a more proper idea of the schematic nature of this Great Basin country one should rather take a handful of pencils of many varying lengths and thicknesses and place them randomly on a table top, while keeping them all pointed in the same direction. What one would then have is a sort of maze made out of pencils, and if one can just imagine the pencils to be up-thrust mountain ranges and the spaces between them river valleys and desert basins, one has a rough approximation of what is meant by a basin-and-range type of topography.

From studying our little schematic model, it should be quite obvious that if the pencil-mountains are all pointing north-south, then any travel in a north-south direction would be relatively easy—one could just proceed from one valley to another paralleling it by just making a slight jog in one's course. On the other hand, any travel in an east-west direction would be at right angles to the axes of these mountains and would require either an endless succession of mountain and valley crossings or a very circuitous sort of journey in order to attempt to skirt around the various mountain ranges. And if it hadn't been for the truly remarkable fact that right through the midst of this country of north-south mountains meandered an east-west flowing river, the Humboldt, this sort of laborious or roundabout route, was exactly what the emigrants would have had to follow. Ironically enough, it was the presence of the much maligned Humboldt that was to make the California Trail a possibility and a reality.

In addition to the fortuitous and strategically placed Humboldt, two other major geologic factors have to be considered in order to understand the nature of physical challenge presented to the emigrant by this curious land. The first of these has to do with the geologic past of the region and the fact that at one time this was an area of much heavier precipitation. Not only was there more rainfall, but during the Pleistocene Era (beginning one million years ago), because of fundamental changes in climate, great glaciers both grew and receded in the Sierra Nevada. Waters from these melting glaciers accumulated in the desert basins and formed a series of sizable freshwater lakes.

Finally these waters reached such depths that they overflowed through their adjoining passes to form one gigantic inland sea. Geologists have named this great prehistoric body of water Lake Lahontan, and at one time it covered over nine thousand square miles. It is around the shores of this vanished lake that the remains of the first human inhabitants of this region have been found. The level of this lake fluctuated considerably over the centuries, but slowly a drying trend set in, and the waters evaporated faster than they refilled. Eventually the one huge lake became a series of smaller ones again, of which the last two are Walker Lake and Pyramid Lake. Other lake bottoms became alkali flats and the various sinks that the emigrants found so curious and so difficult to contend with.

But no geologic feature had (or has) such a complete effect, both directly and indirectly, on the land through which the California Trail passed as the Sierra Nevada. The mountains of this range are another example of the same sort of uptilted granite that we have already seen in the basin-and-range region. The difference, of course, is the difference in the size and scale of this great block. Imagine a mass of granite 90 to 100 miles wide and 400 miles long, pushed up to heights above 14,000 feet along its eastern escarpment, and extending to below the level of the sea for thousands of feet under the thick sediments of the Great Valley of California! It is truly one of the great mountain ranges of the world, and it stood directly in the emigrants' path. "The Elephant's Back" is what the emigrants called it, and they saw it as a truly fierce and exotic creature to be subdued. It was the culminating challenge of the entire trip; it was not just a physical entity, but a psychological one, too.

Not only was the Sierra a barrier to the emigrants coming west, but it also served as a barrier to eastward movement of the moisture-laden storms that came in out of the Pacific. It was this fact that dictated the weather and climate—and consequently the vegetation and much of the topography—of the basin-and-range region. Because of the "rain shadow" effect of the Sierra crest, the emigrant was under its effective dominion almost from the moment of leaving the Oregon Trail. Except for some of the higher mountain ranges (the Ruby Mountains of eastern Nevada are over 11,000 feet), which can catch those small amounts of moisture that slip past the Sierra and so have appreciable snowfalls and rains, there is little precipitation to sustain anything but desert flora. There are forests consisting mainly of piñon pines and desert junipers on the higher mountains and cottonwoods along the river bottoms, but for almost the entire trip across Nevada, the emigrant saw little besides brushy willows, sagebrush, greasewood, and rabbitbrush. Grass was restricted to the river margins, to the marshy regions of the lower Humboldt, and to the numerous springs, both hot and cold, found along the route.

Indeed, aside from a few stretches of hard pulling and the notably difficult descent into Goose Creek, the basin-and-range region of the trail was not all that bad. It might take some time and some looking, but food for the stock was usually to be found, and the lifesaving Humboldt, though tedious and exasperating in its dust, heat, and windings, was a good enough road. It was rather from the region of the sink westward that the really crucial challenges were met.

First came the deserts, and no matter which route might be chosen to leave the Humboldt—whether by Lassen's Cutoff or the Truckee or Carson routes—there were equally long, waterless stretches of hard pulling to be achieved before adequate water could be found. It was on these dry *jornadas* that most of the property and stock were lost and the emigrants suffered the most themselves. Then came some difficult going up the river channels and lower canyons of Sierran rivers, matched by some equally hard marches along the northern routes. But the desert was behind and sources of water were always at hand. It merely became a question of working one's wagon ever upwards along the eastward-flowing courses of rivers and streams until the main backbone of the Sierra was reached. From there followed the truly prodigious effort of assaulting the Sierra crest itself, followed by the unexpectedly long and dangerous descent through the heavily-forested, boulder-strewn ridges and canyons of the seemingly never-ending western slopes.

Thus it was that the emigrant, in a relatively short distance and much compressed period of time, went from the bad water and alkali dust of high desert, to the chill of alpine meadow, to the greenery of temperate forest, to the aridness of low-lying river plain, and from 4,000 feet to nearly 10,000 feet to sea level. It was a prodigious and, for some, and exhilarating experience.

Certainly the emotional high point of the entire journey was the cresting of the Sierra at the various passes. These passes ranged anywhere from 5,200 feet at Beckwourth Pass to 9,500 feet at the second summit on the Carson Route, but the real difficulty was not so much a question of the altitude as of the nature of the eastern side of the Sierra. Donner Pass, for instance, was roughly a thousand feet above the starting point at Donner Lake, and this distance had to be climbed in less than two miles. It was simply an impossible pull for a single wagon and team and required either a community effort of double-teaming or the necessity of leading the teams up separately and then carrying the wagons up piece-by-piece for reassembly at the top. The Donner Pass Route was soon abandoned for a somewhat longer Coldstream Route, but even here the last few hundred yards to the summit required the same sort of procedure. No route was without its disadvantages, and there were plenty of sweat and curses expended on each.

In the end, the crucial factor in deciding just which trail and pass to take boiled down to a question of where the individual emigrant or the majority of his wagon train wanted to be when the Great Central Valley of California was reached. A little harder pull here or there on the eastern side had to be weighed against long days of extra travel on the farther slope. To the earlier emigrants, as to the gold-seeking hordes of 1849 and later, all other things being equal, the shortest route to one's destination had to be considered the best one. The land could challenge, but it couldn't deny.

# the trail

The California Trail snaked its way like a great, recumbent vine across 750 sinuous miles of what is now Idaho, Utah, Nevada, and California. It was an iron-tough, weather-beaten species of desert vine whose tenacious roots gathered in their sustenance from the westward-percolating emigrant waters that flowed from the Oregon and Salt Lake trails. These roots, in turn, gathered into a single, alkali-whitened trunk, which swelled and writhed through the parched country along the Humboldt River before splitting into two main branches at Great Meadows and sending many tendrils and branchlets curling across the high rock wall of the Sierra to finally leaf and bloom upon the sunny slopes of the Pacific.

By any standard, this extraordinary vine was a curious sort of historico-botanical specimen. Indeed, even if Baron von Humboldt, that esteemed and distinguished naturalist whose name was attached to so many of this vine's most memorable and salient features, had actually set eyes upon it, he would have been hard pressed to commit it to record as a meticulously precise, definitive drawing in some historical flora of the West. To be sure, all the various parts of this curious plant were eventually assembled to make it into a taxonomical entity, but it would take some years for those separate parts to be arranged into a final, complete image. It was simply a vine that did not grow by the normal organic progression of seed to seedling to logically matured plant, but rather it was discovered a part at a time and then pieced into a final picture, like some giant jigsaw puzzle. It is with this vine-puzzle and its various historical pieces that we must now briefly concern ourselves.

The first emigrant wagon train to California, known as the Bidwell-Bartleson Party, set out for the unknown in the spring of 1841. John Bidwell himself recalls for us most vividly their lack of understanding as to what lay ahead of them in the next few months of travel:

"Our ignorance of the route was complete. We knew that California lay west, and that was the extent of our knowledge. Some of the maps consulted, supposed of course to be correct, showed a lake in the vicinity of where Salt Lake now is; it was represented as a long lake, three or four hundred miles in extent, narrow and with two outlets, both running into the Pacific Ocean, either apparently larger than the Mississippi River. An intelligent man with whom I boarded—Elam Brown, who till recently lived in California, dying when over ninety years of age—possessed a map that showed these rivers to be large, and he advised me to take tools along to make canoes, so that if we found the country so rough that we could not get along with our wagons we could descend one of those rivers to the Pacific. Even Frémont knew nothing about Salt Lake until 1843, when for the first time he explored it and mapped it correctly, his report being first printed, I think, in 1845."

With such abounding and potentially disastrous misinformation, the Bidwell group followed the already established Oregon Trail to a point just beyond Soda Springs in Idaho. From there they broke a new trail down the Bear River and then westward across the desert region north of Salt Lake. They ran into serious trouble in this desert, and it was only by abandoning their wagons and resorting to pack animals that they were able to make their way across the mountains and along the South Fork to the main stem of the Humboldt. Their contribution to the future California Trail began here, as they broke trail as far as the great sink. Their route from the sink, across the Sierra and into California has never been established beyond all doubt, but it is generally thought that they crossed the crest in the vicinity of Sonora Pass. Neither their approach to the Humboldt River nor their route upon leaving it was to figure in later emigrant routes.

In 1842 there were no additions to the trail because there were no wagon trains to California, but in 1843 the Chiles-Walker Party established the basic Raft River–Goose Creek–Thousand Springs Creek approach to the Humboldt. Their group, running short on supplies, split up a short distance west of Fort Hall on the Oregon Trail. Chiles and a group of men traveled fast and light as far north as Fort Boise and then southwestward through unknown country to Sutter's Fort in California to get supplies for the main wagon train; meanwhile Walker led the wagon train south off the

Oregon Trail at the Port-Neuf River to the Raft River and on to the Humboldt. Unfortunately, the planned rendezvous of the two groups at the sink was not possible, because Chiles and his party reached Sutter's too late in the season to make the necessary eastward crossing of the Sierra. Walker waited a few days and then set off to the south along the eastern flank of the Sierra toward the easy pass he had discovered several years before. Again, food shortages and the slow pace of the wagons forced his party to abandon them in the vicinity of Owens Lake and to continue on by packing. They eventually did cross over into the Central Valley of California and were reunited with Chiles and the other group.

Thus, by the end of 1843, the California Trail was established from the Raft River in Idaho to the sink of the Humboldt, but there was still no route across the Sierra, and no wagons had as yet made it all the way through from the States. It was left for the Stevens Party of 1844 to establish a feasible route through the central Sierra and, in the spring of 1845, to finally bring their marooned wagons down from the Sierra and into the Great Valley. They were assisted in choosing a route for approaching and crossing the Sierra by Sarah Winnemucca's grandfather, Chief Truckee, who gave them a friendly welcome at the sink. They crossed the Forty-mile Desert and followed the Truckee River up its course to Truckee's Lake (Donner Lake). At this point the party split, with one group following up the main course of the Truckee River to Lake Tahoe and then across the mountains via the Rubicon and American rivers, while the main group took the route that was later to be known as the Donner Trail via Donner Lake and Donner Pass. At the lake they were forced by snow to leave part of their wagons, and eventually one young member of their party, Moses Schallenberger, spent the winter by himself in a cabin at the lake. In the spring of 1845 both the wagons and young Moses were retrieved, and a passage of the central Sierra achieved. It could be done.

It only remained for the wagon train of 1845 to establish that the whole continental trek could be achieved in one season. Led by the old mountain man and guide Caleb Greenwood, who had covered the route with the Stevens Party in 1844 and hurried east in the spring to offer his services as a guide, the emigrants of this year avoided the difficult and time-consuming canyon of the Truckee above Reno and made the crossing of the summit without undue hardship. The thing was proven beyond any doubt: the whole two-thousand-mile journey could indeed be made safely in one season. The road to California was open.

After the triumph of 1845, the route was merely improved and alternatives added. The year 1846 saw Donner Pass generally abandoned for a longer and higher crossing just to the south via Coldstream Canyon. Eastward-traveling Mormons opened a new route over Carson Pass (Chiles, in late 1846, extended it to the sink region), which was destined to become the most popular of all the crossings. It was also in this year that Hastings established his route south of Salt Lake via the South Fork to the main Humboldt—the route of the ill-fated Donner Party. And finally, this was the year in which the Applegate scouting party opened up their route to southern Oregon from the Great Meadows on the Humboldt

*Bruff's winter camp above Mill Creek was thirty-odd miles from the end of Lassen's Trail.*

via Black Rock Desert—a route that was to become part of the future Lassen and Nobles' trails.

In 1848 the whole of the Lassen Trail was plotted (to get heavy use in '49), and a trail north from the Mormon settlement at Salt Lake was brought into the original California Trail just west of the City of Rocks. The year 1849 saw the addition of the much used Hudspeth's Cutoff, which struck almost due west from Soda Springs and thus made unnecessary the swing to the north and Fort Hall. This cutoff joined the original trail at Cassia Creek east of the City of Rocks.

By the end of the great Gold Rush year of 1849, the three main routes for crossing the Sierra—Donner, Carson, and Lassen—were fully established. To these, three other main routes of later discovery should be added: Beckwourth's (1851), Nobles' (1852), and Sonora (1852). These routes were developed partly from a natural desire to find easier routes across the Sierra, but also in a large measure from the desire of the many new towns in the gold regions of the foothills to see emigrant traffic funneled their way. Nobles' and Beckwourth's routes were relatively easy and took newcomers into the northern gold fields; the Sonora route was not easy, but led directly to the southern fields. In the decades of the fifties and sixties, both Nobles' and Beckwourth's routes were used by large numbers of emigrants and to bring large herds of cattle into California. The Sonora Route acquired a bad reputation and only a trickle of emigrants made it their choice.

Finally, two other routes for crossing the Sierra should be mentioned to make the record complete, because each of them had some considerable use during certain periods before they lost out in the competition with the older routes. The first was the Henness Pass Route via the Little Truckee, which had considerable use in the sixties because of a local gold rush. It had the advantage of a very easy approach from the normally difficult eastern side, but its western slopes were just as difficult and tedious as any other, and it was destined to lose out completely when both the road and the railroad through the Sierra Nevada were plotted just to the south at Donner Pass.

The other route came to be known as the Big Trees Trail and was really just a branch off of the popular Carson Trail. It left the Carson Trail, continued south up Hope Valley and on up Faith and Charity valleys, then crossed over to the Calaveras Big Trees and down the ridge between the Stanislaus and Mokelumne watersheds to the southern gold fields. It became a much traveled wagon route in the 1850s and '60s.

One further thing should be given some attention as we close this brief historical survey of the development of the California Trail and go on to consider the various sections in more detail. This trail, like almost all the others in the history of the westward expansion of the United States, was not opened under the auspices of the federal government but through the combined efforts of individual emigrants. This was not government on the move, but *people* on the move, and the distinction is of considerable importance in understanding this period in American history. In a very real sense, Washington could only ratify what its people presented to it as accomplished fact. It was a time when individual action could directly affect national policy and did. As Edwin Bryant was to note in 1846, upon meeting the Applegate exploration contingent on the Humboldt:

"I could not, however, but reflect upon and admire the public spirit and enterprise of the small band of men from whom we had just parted. Our government, doubtless, has been desirous of exploring and pointing out the most favorable routes to the Pacific, and has appropriated large sums of money for this purpose. But whatever has been accomplished in the way of explorations, which is of much practical utility, has resulted from the indomitable energy, the bold daring, and the unconquerable enterprise, in opposition to every discouragement, privation, and danger, of our hardy frontier men and pioneers, unaided directly or remotely by the patronage or even the approving smiles and commendations of the government. To them we are indebted for the originally discovered wagon-route to Oregon and California, and to them we are indebted for all the valuable improvements, and *cut-offs* on this route. To them we are indebted for a good, well-beaten, and plain trail to the Pacific ocean, on the shores of which, in the face of almost insurmountable difficulties, unsupported, they have founded an empire. Let us honor those to whom honor is due."

# THE HERITAGE
# OF THE
# CALIFORNIA TRAIL

"August 30.—After travelling some three or four miles rising and descending a number of hills, from the summit of one more elevated than the others surrounding it, the spacious valley of the Sacramento suddenly burst upon my view, at an apparent distance of fifteen miles. A broad line of timber running through the centre of the valley indicated the course of the main river, and smaller and fainter lines on either side of this, winding through brown and flat plain, marked the channels of its tributaries. I contemplated this most welcome scene with such emotions of pleasure as may be imagined by those who have ever crossed the desert plains and mountains of western America, until Jacob, who was in advance of the remainder of the party, came within the reach of my voice. I shouted to him that we were 'out of the woods' to pull off his hat and give three cheers, so loud that those in the rear could hear them. Very soon the huzzas of those behind were ringing and echoing through the hills, valleys, and forests, and the whole party came up with an exuberance of joy in their motions and depicted upon their countenances. It was a moment of cordial and heartfelt congratulations."

As the emigrants climbed that final hill and saw before them at long last the Great Valley of California, rare, indeed, would be the person amongst them who did not feel that same rush of exuberance, that same spark of exaltation, that same flush of triumph which Bryant's journal recorded for us in 1846. They had dared it, and they had prevailed! It was a truly grand and historic journey drawn to a successful close. A continent had been traversed and a magnificent human effort ended, an effort in which the daily obstacles were not just the rocks and rivers and mountains and canyons of the exterior environment, but also the fears and frustrations and anger and various other features of the interior, psychological landscape.

The whole journey had been from the first the most personal of experiences, and the emigrants adopted a significant phrase from the jargon of the day to give proper emphasis to the immensity of the undertaking as they saw it. They referred to the great challenge itself as "the elephant." The choice of term was not only metaphorically inspired, but it was also highly significant. After all, the elephant was a living thing. It was the greatest, most awesome, most fantastic, most fearsome of all the land beasts. It was truly the ultimate expression of Nature's creative imagination. Very few of these emigrants had ever seen a real elephant, but that did not matter. This was pure hyperbole; this was a personification of what each felt within himself. The important thing was not that such a fabled beast might or did actually exist but that they were willing to go and see if it did. They would commit themselves to go "to see the elephant," and they would find it and challenge it and master it, or they would die in the trying.

They had no illusions about the thing. They knew that they were putting their very lives in the balance in this trip across the continent. The stakes were as personal and fundamental as that. But this act of theirs was far more than just a personal undertaking, just an individual commitment; this matter of the elephant was also a *human* challenge and, ultimately, a triumph for humanity. The victory, while won one person at a time, was a generic one; it was a victory over all the elephantine obstacles that a still-supreme Nature could contrive to put in nineteenth-century man's way.

We have already discussed in general terms just who these emigrants were who dared "to see the elephant." We have talked of why they came, of how they came, and of where they went. We know that they made the decision to undertake this arduous journey for a myriad of personal reasons and that they came as individuals, as families, as groups. They came as part of the ever-continuing westward expansion of the nation, and they carried with them the ideals of law and social order, the customs, the religious traditions, the political and economic forms of the republic from which they had voluntarily chosen to emigrate.

Some probably couldn't have cared less that they were leaving the United States behind; some regretted it but for their own reasons left anyway; some had no intention at all of leaving their nation behind—they openly proposed to carry it right along with them. But whatever were the private thoughts, motivations, and intentions of these emigrants, the net result was that, as a group, they succeeded in insuring the expansion of the republic into a continental nation.

Most emigrants at least suspected that they were participating in a small way in a historic event (it can be seen in their writings and in their actions; it was openly emblazoned in various patriotic slogans on their wagon covers), but it would certainly be a misapprehension to view this westward movement as some sort of great, purposeful conspiracy or crusade. The thing was really much more subtle than that—if one can accept the thought of wagons rolling through the desert as being subtle at all. These emigrants were just doing what came naturally to them; they were simply so many individually-minded persons joining together to achieve a common undertaking, as had been the tradition of the republic from its earliest days. It was only by such a joining together that the individual could attempt and succeed in such an audacious endeavor as crossing some two thousand miles of largely unknown wilderness in search of a new life and home.

All this had little to do with overt governmental policy. This was no national goal sent down from officials on high. Of course, the federal government was not ignorant of what was going on, and it was expressing its own expansionistic proclivities with the war with Mexico and the challenge to England over the Oregon Territory, but this was not the motivating factor. The emigrant was truly on his own. It was fine with him if the government chose to follow (and there seemed to be the tacit expectation on both parts that it would do just that), but basically it was a question of the flag following the people and not vice versa. This was to be another of those spontaneous, grass-roots expressions of one of the most salient and characteristic facets of American life: the desire and freedom to move on in an attempt to change and, hopefully, improve one's lot.

It was in this very process of seeking out the goal of personal satisfaction and individual fulfillment that the physical barrier of the western wilderness was first breached and then conquered. And in the very performance of that monumental accomplishment, the emigrant contributed to the growth and perpetuation of a certain national ethos, which had come to him from his own pioneering forebears and has been passed on to us as part of our common heritage right down to this day. It has to do with the fundamental perception of the nature of man's relationship to his environment.

To the emigrant, as it has been for most of the history of mankind, it was not a relationship that left him the luxury of options. The sole purpose of life was to survive, and to survive was to wage an unrelenting war with the forces of Nature. Pretechnological man didn't question that hard fact; it was the simple, cold necessity that man prevail. The margin between life and death was always so thin that there could be no room for passivity; the battle was unending.

Against this background of never-ending conflict between man and Nature, a corollary thought began to establish itself, which posited that since Nature was to be viewed as a threatening, out-and-out enemy (or at very best a capricious, destructive force), then it directly followed that Nature itself was to be used in any manner that would benefit man or give him the advantage in his struggle to survive. After all, this was war, and one need have no qualms in plundering the foe and using this plunder to fight him. That sort of thing was to be expected. Nature gave no quarter, and man would give no quarter.

It might well be that from time to time a truce might be declared, and then the artist or the poet or the philosopher might feel free to rhapsodize on Nature—there was, after all, beauty to be found in the beast—and civilized man could give expression to the aesthetic side of his own nature if he should so desire. For instance, it was perfectly all right for the emigrant along the California Trail to see that the desert could have its moments of rare beauty, its hours of restful tranquility, but it was always to be recognized as the potential enemy, and these moments of pleasure were to be considered mirages masking the real peril that was always there. The desert destroyed; the desert killed; beware! The desert was a place to be passed through quickly, and what was there that was of use to man was to be used and used fully and without question. Then, when all use was gone, it was to be casually left behind and forgotten.

Need—need and use: these were the two considerations that had to be applied in evaluating the worth of any part of the emigrant's physical environment. These two imperatives were the basis of the pioneer ethos, and they remained valid for all of mankind right up until that time—*our* time—when man was able to establish a parity, if not a tenuous hegemony, vis-à-vis Nature. It was always the priority of *survival* that mattered in such simple and unsophisticated times. Wilderness and the land were a threat to that survival just as surely as early frosts, high waters, hostile Indians, and the cholera were threats. There was no choice but to do battle with this awesome array of foes and to use any and all of the mind's and the land's own resources to assure the perpetuation of the human species. Nature was to be conquered; the treasures of the land were to be taken and used; man's complete dominion over the earth was to be established; it was an injunction that had biblical authority. Given the context of the times, it was a national ethos that was entirely proper because it was entirely necessary.

This book has been a sympathetic attempt to re-create in word and picture the mood and flavor of that time in our nation's history when the challenge of the West was at its romantic and mysterious peak and the American emigrant set out to conquer it for himself and, indirectly, for his nation. The 1840s and 1850s were times of great excitement for our nation —times of war, times of boom, and times of depression, times of rapid and sometimes painful internal growth and experimentation, times when the republic was feeling its youthful pride, when issues and pressures were inexorably building toward that great testing of the capacity of the adolescent nation to hold itself together. It was a time when many of the basic values and rationales and formulations of our way of life were being tested and shaped and gropingly articulated. It was a frenetic, vibrant, exciting time, and it was to leave its mark on our national character.

We have here been concerned with only one particularly fascinating aspect to those times—the California Trail. We have been concerned with the written record and with the record as it remains expressed upon the land. The written record has been pretty much preserved, but the story as recorded on the land is in serious danger of being irretrievably lost when, with but a little concern and effort, it too could be forever preserved.

It is not enough, therefore, to simply let the matter end in soporific reveries and the heady incense of nostalgia—at least not if one is truly interested in our nation's historical heritage. It is entirely proper for us to look back and savor the past, but we must live in the present and think to the future. And when one does face the present, one is struck with the irony of the fact that the old ethos which controlled the emigrant's attitude toward the land is still very much alive and active in our contemporary laws and public morality, and is bidding fair to destroy the last tenuous impressions on the land of those selfsame emigrants.

It is a sad thing to witness, if only for the reason that the pattern of thinking about and approaching Nature that was a necessity to them has for the most part become a matter of choice for us. We do not have to approach Nature as an enemy to be battled to the very end; we do not have to attack the land and use all its resources just because they are there to be exploited; we do not have to conquer and tame all our physical surroundings; we do not have to approach the problem burdened and perverted by a mentality that has outlived its time. Indeed, all the indications are that if we continue to practice this extension of the pioneer ethos into these technologically advanced times, we will run the serious risk of greatly reducing the quality of life and even of making much of our planet sterile and unlivable.

We indisputably have the means to change the basic rules of the age-old conflict between man and Nature; what we need now is a new environmental ethos to control and direct those means. There are sensible alternatives and choices open to us in these matters right now, and we need to make those choices on the basis of what we are and want for ourselves in our *own* times.

In this regard, we must always keep in mind that modern technology is a fully two-headed beast—its voracious appetite for ever-increasing amounts of energy and natural resources can easily chain us forever to the outdated and rapacious ethos of expediency, or it can be directed to the end of providing us with the luxury and privilege of pursuing new alternatives and solutions and of picking out of this land and its heritage just exactly what we *choose* to preserve and conserve along the way. If we don't purposely guide it, it will surely end up dominating us.

We must simply face up to the fact that times have changed, new conditions have arisen, new values and new rationales and new expectations have come into being, and that, consequently, new formulations of public policies have to be forthcoming. Choices, even choices long sanctified on the basis of an inherited public ethos, have to be reexamined from time to time on the basis of new life-styles and new life-needs. Not every period of time, not every generation, is faced with the necessity of dealing with such a fundamental reassessment of national values and priorities. Some times are more comfortable and easy to live in than others. It is quite possible to be content to live happily with the rationales worked out by previous generations. Indeed, the tendency of human nature is to do just that—we just let things go along as they always have; we just let inertia carry us along as best it will until we bump into something that shakes us out of our lethargy.

Well, such bucolic times are not for us. Whether we like it or not, we are in the throes of one of those intense and uncomfortable periods of time in which there must be a thorough reassessment of fundamental national values, and the direction in which we are to go is far from certain.

One of the basic causes of this indecision is that the old pioneer ethos is still very much alive in our society, even though it is pathetically out-dated. The age-old concept that man and Nature must do constant and unrelenting battle if man is to survive is just not valid in a technologically advanced society in which changed social conditions and institutions practically guarantee one's physical survival, no matter what. It is no longer the imperative matter of keeping people alive, but rather a question of keeping people at work in a welfare-minded, affluent society. And further than that, it is a question of keeping that society affluent in the face of finite and ever-dwindling supplies of natural energy sources.

The trouble with trying to solve this very difficult part of the problem is that it brings us right up against one of those crucial conflicts so inherent to our system of life. On the one hand we want to preserve the traditional ideals concerning the rights of the individual, while at the same time we are being forced more and more to recognize that we can only preserve some measure of meaningful individual choice in life by seeing to it that individual interests can no longer divert to themselves the constantly dwindling reservoir or the *public* treasure. Inescapably, we are faced with the contradictory need of *community* control—both locally and nation-ally—to preserve even the possibility of *individual* choices.

This sort of contradiction is, of course, nothing new to our system; there has always been this tension between individual rights and the public good, and the Constitution itself spells out the rules under which this tension is played out. But the Constitution expresses and defines things in terms of political and social relationships; it doesn't deal with the modern problem of individual rights as related to the environment and natural resources. It didn't have to do so because it was beyond all con-ception to the eighteenth-century mind that the seemingly boundless natural resources of the nation could ever be reduced to the point that priorities would have to be set for their use. The right to private property and the legal use of it to one's own purposes were enshrined high on the altar of constitutional rights because, like God Himself, the natural domain was conceived to be infinite. There was always more of every physical resource to be had out West. This was a land of infinite plenty, and the individual was to be free to take whatever he needed or wanted of that plenty. And what was true for the private sector could only be presumed to hold true for the public sector. There was no Bill of Rights for the land or the environment; such a thing was preposterous!

It is no longer preposterous. We must redefine the rights of the individual in terms of the environment. We simply have no choice. The time for this has come, just as the time has come to reassert the public's right to the public domain. After two hundred years of the most extravagant use of our land and exploitation of its resources and energy sources, we know that the "infinite" of yesteryear is, indeed, most finite today. The land and its resources must be used intelligently, and what can be spared from use and preserved for aesthetic and historical reasons must be purposely set aside and protected, or it will simply disappear under the pressure of population and energy needs.

Certain portions of the land deserve to be set aside in perpetuity to be cherished and protected *as they are*. Otherwise choice is gone, freedom is gone, options are meaningless, and the concept of the individual's right to "life, liberty, and the pursuit of happiness" is so circumscribed by the actual condition of the land as to be a hollow and gratuitous mockery. And it is not just a question of *our* rights and *our* choices and *our* freedoms, but it is also a question of the rights and choices and freedoms of all generations to come.

This is really what the conservation and preservation movement in our time is all about. It is basically concerned with the disposition of the vast *public* domain, and it does not seek to take away anyone's individual access and use of that land *except* when that use is destructive of its intrinsic value to the nation.

The conservation movement is often belittled and condemned (by those who see their own interests threatened somehow by its interference) for wanting to "lock up" the entire nation's resources for the selfish enjoyment (and a merely aesthetic enjoyment at that!) of a few. Actually, what the conservationists seek to do is to see to it that the special-interest groups don't plunder every reachable, mineable, grazeable portion of the public domain before it can be considered for preservation for its own intrinsic worth.

These would-be exploiters of all the public treasure are by no means evil men. They are usually very sincere, honest men who are providing jobs and goods for the nation. The trouble is that far too often they are men and corporations who still think and act under the spell of a public ethos which no longer fits our times. They tend to be nineteenth-century men with twentieth-century technology at their disposal, and the combination is both dangerous and frightening, for they can do more damage to the land in a day than the emigrant man could ever do.

These men rail against the conservationists for "locking up" the nation's resources while at the selfsame time they choose to ignore the fact that if they had their way, there would very shortly be nothing left to lock up. Certainly it is a lock-up of sorts, but by definition that which is locked away can be unlocked if need be. What is gone, is gone forever.

With a few minor exceptions, there have been no "locks" put on the California Trail at all. That it exists at all is simply due to the fact that along many of its desert stretches the land use over the years has been such that it chanced to survive. It has persisted despite the neglect of those private groups who should be interested in its preservation and the benign indifference of those federal agencies who are charged with its supervision. It exists as an accident of topography, and one might well ask why it can't be left that way. Why can't the desert and physical remoteness continue to play the role of guardian?

It would be a happy thing if such could remain the case, but unfortunately, the fortuitous happenstance of isolation is not likely to preserve this part of our historical heritage much longer. The insatiable demand for new energy sources is causing an ever-increasing interest in the thermal regions along the trail, and the need for minerals has led to highly visible prospecting in the mountains beyond. It is already impossible to go anywhere in large areas of Nevada and not find every vista scarred by the prospector's bulldozer and pitted with sample holes. Soon it will be the drilling derrick, the steel tower, the concrete building, and the asphalt road screening out the historic hot springs. There is no doubt that something very material will be gained by this march of civilization—jobs and wealth—but in the process, something more fragile and precious—history and beauty—will be lost forever.

If the sacrifice were truly necessary to the well-being of the nation, then few thinking persons would question the loss, although they might mourn it. But the sad truth is that decisions of this sort concerning the public domain are not made on the basis of any national priorities set up to consider legitimate alternative uses of the land. This is not in any way a plea against development of jobs and natural resources; it most certainly is a plea for a balanced and intelligent program of priorities in land use. There are many areas of thermal activity in the West which could be explored and developed before those of historic importance need be exploited; there are many mineralized mountain ranges throughout the Great Basin Region that could be given priority for development. Let us meet our needs in those regions first, and *then*—if future conditions make it necessary—let us have final resort to these areas which have significance to us as a nation.

This sort of approach will, of course, require that the federal government establish a well-defined and all-inclusive policy of national priorities for land in the public domain, a policy in which environmental impact will be clearly expanded to include such considerations as historical and aesthetic value. We can afford as a nation to have just such an enlightened policy and through its use bring the public domain out from under the control of special interests and back under public control and public scrutiny. Much of the physical heritage of the California Trail has already been lost; some is, unquestionably, beyond the public's control; some is only newly threatened; none need be further sacrificed if a reasonable policy is established to protect that which is still so very easy to protect.

Of course, no effort at conservation and preservation ever is easy. There are always too many special interests and divergent attitudes toward what constitutes the public good. And it will be a struggle of no mean proportions before the pioneer ethos ceases to dominate much of the thinking here in the West. Several very large and crucial battles will have to be won before a new and enlightened environmental ethos can take its place. A fully comprehensive policy on land-use priorities will have to be established. The disgraceful and archaic Mining Law of 1872, which after one hundred years and only cosmetic changes is still the basic law on mining of the public domain, must be completely rewritten to reflect the environmental ethos of *our* times. The federal Bureau of Land Management must be adequately funded and manned and given proper direction for their stewardship of the public lands. The mining and grazing interests, who too often assume an attitude of proprietory rights over certain portions of the public domain, must be brought to realize that their use of this part of the public treasure is just a privilege and nothing more.

And, finally, the public must be brought to realize the vast extent of the public domain and must be encouraged to take a direct interest in the future use of that domain.

On a less grandiose and more immediate level, there are some actions which should be taken now to preserve the California Trail. A moratorium on development along the trail should be declared by the Bureau of Land Management wherever it has jurisdiction until such a time as the historical worth of the various areas has been established. The City of Rocks in Idaho and Black Rock Desert and High Rock Canyon in Nevada are areas demanding to be set aside from the public domain for protection. If for some bureaucratic reason they can not be designated as primitive areas or national historic monuments, then they should receive some special protective designation from Congress. There are many areas of the Sierra which should be promptly protected and set aside by the Forest Service.

There is much else that could and should be done, but the truth of the matter is that none of these things *will* get done unless local and state historical organizations, interested conservation groups, and ordinary citizens become interested in the preservation of the California Trail and insist that the various governmental agencies concerned do something about it. Apathy added to bureaucracy is a fatal combination.

The heritage of the California Trail is both historical and scenic. It is a part of our country's story which can and should be preserved. It should not be locked up and stored away like some priceless heirloom book. That part that is on the land deserves to be seen, to be studied, to be enjoyed and appreciated. But, at the same time, it is a fragile record, a unique record, and if it is lost, it is lost forever. It needs to be cherished and loved and protected (from friend and from enemy, from over-use and misuse) as all important things in life do. If we don't do it now, it simply won't be there for another more thoughtful and appreciative generation to do. We either pass it on as a physical presence, or it will disappear leaving only the written record. It is as simple as that.

To our California-bound forebears, moving westward under the wisdom and ethos of *their* times, the land through which they labored was something to conquer and tame and use. Is it to remain just that to us in *our* times, or will it become a heritage to honor and cherish and preserve?

# A PICTORIAL JOURNEY

Rabbithole Springs, Nevada

Hoarfrost—Cassia Creek, Idaho

THE MAIN TRUNK TRAIL TO CALIFORNIA originally branched off from the Snake River and the Oregon Trail at Raft River in south-central Idaho (albeit slightly eastward of this point for the pioneering Walker contingent of 1843). In 1848, a trail was pushed north from the Mormon settlements at Salt Lake to join this Raft River route just west of the City of Rocks, and in 1849, Hudspeth's Cutoff linked up to it at Cassia Creek just east of the City of Rocks. Thus, there was just one trail from the vicinity of the City of Rocks westward, and the vast majority of emigrants over the years funneled into and traveled along this northerly route to California.

The City of Rocks was not only a sort of geographical hub for the California Trail, but it was also one of the great scenic features of the journey. The name itself derived from the fancied resemblance of this marvelous assemblage of granite rocks and domes and spires to some mysterious, frozen city, as conjured up in the imaginations of the emigrants. Together with Independence Rock and Devil's Gate—both far to the east on the Oregon Trail—this memorable "city" of silent stone elicited as much comment in the writings of the emigrants as any feature along the entire route, and most justifiably so. It is certainly the scenic high point of this section of trail, which includes such other notable features as the strikingly colored cliffs of Goose Creek and that varied conglomeration of curiously propertied waters gushing from a canyon wall that gave Thousand Springs Valley its name.

This first section of the California Trail was generally lacking in difficult topographical barriers. With the exception of some mountainous terrain followed by the dangerous descent into Goose Creek, the trail was generally good, and except for the normal amount of pilferage and the customary number of "night scares," the Shoshones were not all that troublesome. The impression one gets from the various journals is that this was a fairly relaxed period for the traveler. These were halcyon days—the country was interesting, the grass and water sufficient if not plentiful, the Indians quiescent, and the morale good. And why not? At last, the direct journey to California had begun!

# The Raft River Approach

Desert wildflower—Raft River, Idaho

Snake River Canyon, Idaho

The banks of the river, for a considerable distance, both above and below the falls, have a volcanic character: masses of basaltic rock are piled one upon another; the water makes its way through their broken chasms, boiling through narrow channels, or pitching in beautiful cascades over ridges of basaltic columns.

Beyond these falls, they came to a picturesque, but inconsiderable stream, called the Cassie. It runs through a level valley, about four miles wide, where the soil is good; but the prevalent coldness and dryness of the climate is unfavorable to vegetation.

Washington Irving,
*Bonneville's Adventures*

Register Rock—Rock Creek, Idaho

*Oct. 14th. . . . I am suspicious that thousands have crossed these tremendous heights the present year, who will not acquire immortal honor by the exploit. One thing, however, is certain; that is, if the names of the California emigrants should not chance to be inscribed in the records of fame, you may yet see countless thousands of their names, very legibly written with chalk, wagon grease, or paint, upon the everlasting rocks that compose the towering ranges of these mountains. Volumes might be filled with these elevated names. Here are monuments that will stand until the "rocks fall to dust," though the inscriptions upon them will soon fade away.*

Franklin Langworthy, 1850

Snake River at Rock Creek, Idaho

Cassia Creek Valley, Idaho

*Saturday July 7. . . . Cash [Cassia] Vally is most beautifully surrounded by high*
*mountains the taller peaks of which are covered with perpetual snows. There are*
*3 creeks putting into this vally from the mountains. . . . We encamped tonight on*
*the center stream where we found plenty of good grass wood and water. . . . About*
*sunset I found my way to the top of one of the nearest peaks, from the top of which*
*I had a most spacious view of the surrounding country. The south side of this*
*peak was covered with seeder & grass, and the top with shivered stone & the North*
*with snow—and the whole with Musketoes.*

James A. Pritchard, 1849

*Tuesday Aug. 14. Morn chilly, raw wind from E. . . . road dusty & heavy as usual.*
*We had been told & had seen notes & cards stating the same thing that it was 100*
*miles to the Humboldt River from the commencement of this cut off. As we had*
*travelled that distance on it we were in hopes today to see that famous river & camp*
*on its banks tonight. When therefore this morning we emerged from the valley where*
*we passed the night upon a broad plain with a line of trees through its center we were*
*sure we saw the Humboldt Valley & consoled ourselves with the reflection that twas*
*only 3 or 4 miles now to the Sierra Nevada & made our calculations how we could*
*reach them in 12 days &c. Judge our disappointment & heartsinking to learn after*
*a hard morning's travelling On reaching "the row of trees" that we were on the head*
*of Raft River, & that twas 130 miles yet to the Humboldt!*

Elisha Perkins, 1849

Wagon traces—City of Rocks, Idaho

City of Rocks, Idaho

Emigrant initials—City of Rocks, Idaho

Aug: 29—An entire range on our left, of volcanic hills, for about 15 miles: and on our right, similar formations for about 10 ms. when we entered a very extraordinary valley, called the "City of Castles." . . . A couple of miles long, and probably ½ mile broad, A light grey decripitating granite, (probably altered by fire) in blocks of every size, from that of a barrel to the dimensions of a large dwelling-house; groups, Masses on Masses, and Cliffs; and worn, by the action of ages of elementary affluences, into strange and romantic forms.—The travellers had marked several large blocks, as their fancy dictated the resemblance to houses, castles, &c.— On one was marked (with tar) "NAPOLEON'S CASTLE," another "CITY HOTEL," &c. We nooned among these curious monuments of nature. I dined hastily, on bread & water, and while others rested, I explored and sketched some of these queer rocks. A group, on left of the trail, resembled gigantic fungii, petrified, other clusters were worn in cells and caverns; and one, which contrasted with the size and hight of the adjacent rocks, seemed no larger than a big chest, was, to my astonishment, when close to it, quite large, hollow, with a arch'd entrance, and capable of containing a dozen persons. . . . This, from its peculiar shape, I named the "Sarcophagus Rock."

J. Goldsborough Bruff, 1849

Table Bluff—Goose Creek, Idaho

*As you enter Goose Creek valley, you will be delighted with its beauty. It contains several table bluffs, mountain-high, with their smooth, level tops, breaking off square at their edges, then gradually and smoothly sloping down to the level of the valley.*

Platt and Slater Guide, 1852

*Monday, August 18th. We passed a chalk bed, likewise some very singular looking rocks on the right hand side of the road. They were all sorts of shaped holes and men had written their names in and under them. The swallows had built numerous nests in them.*

Jane Gould, 1862

Swallow nests—Goose Creek, Idaho

Goose Creek, Idaho

*July 24. . . . After our noon halt we ascended a hill and drove on
to the wild, strange valley of Goose Creek. From the summit of the
hill, a fine and peculiarly interesting view was afforded. It had
evidently been the scene of some violent commotion, appearing as
if there had been a breaking up of the world. Far as the eye could
reach, cones, tables, and nebulae, peculiar to the country, extended
in a confused mass, with many hills apparently white with lime
and melted quartz—some of them of a combination of lime and
sandstone—perhaps it might be called volcanic grit; while others
exhibited, in great regularity, the varied colors of the rainbow.
I have seen the broken hills exhibit, in parallel lines, white, red,
brown, pink, green and yellow, and sometimes a blending of
various colors. It is an interesting field for the geologist, as well
as for the lover of the works of nature.*

Alonzo Delano, 1849

Sunset—Thousand Springs Valley, Nevada

*July 26. . . . At night, a man came to our
camp who had taken a passage at St. Louis
in the Pioneer line of spring wagons, which
were advertised to go through in sixty days.
He was on foot, armed with a knife and
pistol, and carried in a small knapsack all
his worldly goods, except a pair of blankets,
which were rolled up on his shoulders.
He told us that at Willow Springs their
mules gave out, and there was a general
distribution of property, a small portion of
the passengers only obtaining mules, the
rest being obliged to go a thousand miles
without supplies, in the best manner they
could, trusting to luck and the emigrants for
provisions. The passengers had each paid
two hundred dollars for their passage, but
now, like the Irishman on the towpath,
were obliged to work it out. No emigrant
would see him suffer under such circumstances, and we cheerfully shared our
poor fare with him.*

Alonzo Delano, 1849

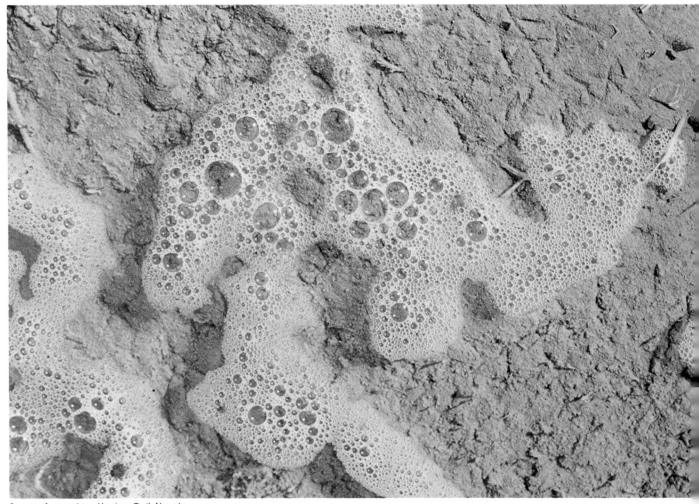

Seepage from spring—Hastings Trail, Nevada

THE SECOND BASIC APPROACH from the east was the Hastings Cutoff, which was opened in 1846. This was the route that came south of Salt Lake and west across the frightful Salt Lake Desert to the East Humboldt and Ruby mountains and the South Fork of the Humboldt. This route was followed by the ill-fated Donner Party, and their subsequent tragedy in the snows of the Sierra made it infamous.

The simple truth of the matter was that there was just too much desert and too little water and grass for this ever to be a feasible route for wagons. There is some evidence, however, that it received light usage in the Gold Rush years of 1849 and after from packers who were intent on moving fast and light, and on winning for themselves an advantage over those more timid souls who stuck to the safer—and thus more crowded—northern routes. Despite its rather ominous reputation for suffering and hardship, there is scant record of an actual excess of fatalities along the Hastings Cutoff; there always seemed to be just enough water and grass to make quick passage possible.

The trail itself came off the salt flats of the Salt Lake Desert and turned southward from the abundant springs at the base of Pilot Peak before striking westward across a series of low mountain ranges and desert valleys, by way of conveniently spaced desert springs. Upon reaching the high East Humboldt Range, the traveler had a choice, depending on his mode of travel. Pack trains could work their way directly across the heights by mountain passes and animal trails, and thus save considerable time and mileage, but wagon trains were forced to detour to the south around the even more lofty Ruby Mountains before swinging north up the course of the South Fork to meet the main trail coming down the Humboldt. The lower course of the South Fork cuts through mountainous terrain and the time needed to force one's way through this difficult canyon caused a great deal of further delay for any who chose this route. Thus, the terrible desert crossing from Salt Lake, the detour around the Ruby Mountains, and the canyon of the South Fork all combined to render this a most unacceptable road for wagon travel.

It is one of the great ironies of the history of

# The Hastings Cutoff

Blazing star—Warm Springs, Nevada

the California Trail that if Hastings had only turned *north* instead of south at the base of the East Humboldt Mountains, he could have reached the headwaters of the main Humboldt —and the main trail to California—by only a day's journey over easy, open country. It would have cut off from his route the nearly two weeks that were lost by detouring around the Ruby Mountains, and (all other things remaining equal, which is perhaps too tenuous a proposition), it would undoubtedly have permitted the Donner contingent to reach and cross the Sierra before snow fell and thus have averted that tragic chapter of western history.

*August 6.—The night was perfectly serene. . . . The moon and the countless starry host of the firmament exhibited their lustrous splendor in a perfection of brilliancy unknown to the night-watchers in the humid regions of the Atlantic; illuminating the numberless mountain peaks rising, one behind the other, to the east, and the illimitable desert of salt that spread its wintry drapery before me, far beyond the reach of the vision, like the vast winding-sheet of a dead world! The night was cold, and kindling a fire of the small, dead willows around the spring, I watched until the rich, red hues of the morning displayed themselves above the eastern horizon, tinging slightly at first, and then deepening in color, the plain of salt, until it appeared like a measureless ocean of vermilion, with here and there a dark speck, the shadow of some solitary buttes, representing islands, rising from its glowing bosom.*

Edwin Bryant, 1846

Desert sunrise—Hastings Trail, Utah

Reeds—Flowery Spring, Nevada

The plain appears to be an almost perfect level,
and is walled in by ranges of mountains on both
sides, running nearly north and south. Wild sage,
greasewood, and a few shrubs of a smaller size,
for the most part leafless, and apparently dead or
dying, are the only vegetation of this valley. . . .

About two o'clock, P.M., after travelling three-
fourths the distance across the valley, we struck an
oasis of about fifty acres of green grass, reeds,
and other herbage, surrounding a number of
springs, some of cool fresh water, others of warm
sulphur water. These waters rise here, and
immediately sink in the sands. . . . The grass
immediately around the springs, although not of
the best quality, is very luxuriant, and on the whole,
it being a favorable place for grazing our mules,—
no apprehensions being entertained of their
straying, or of Indian depredations,—we
determined to encamp for the day. . . .

Mound Springs, Nevada

100

Approach to Snow Water Lake, Nevada

*August 7.—Fifteen miles brought us to the slope of the mountain on the western side of this valley, where we found a bold spring gushing forth a volume of water sufficient to turn the most powerful mill-wheel, but like all the other springs of this desert which we have seen, after running a short distance, the water sinks and disappears in the thristing sands. Around this spring there are a few small willows and a luxuriant growth of grass, with some handsome yellow flowers.*

Edwin Bryant, 1846

Warm Springs, Nevada

Ruby Mountains, Nevada

*August 8.—The morning was clear and cool. A slight dew was perceptible on the grass and on our blankets. Our course to-day was nearly the same as yesterday. We passed over the range of mountains under which we had encamped, by ascending one of its most elevated peaks. When we reached the summit of this peak, after repeatedly stopping on the side of the mountain to breathe our mules, they seemed nearly exhausted and scarcely able to proceed on the journey. The descent on the western side was so steep and difficult, that our animals and ourselves (dismounted of course) slid or jumped down rather than walked.*

Edwin Bryant, 1846

Morning ice on creek—Ruby Mountains, Nevada

Hot spring—Ruby Valley, Nevada

*Aug. 9th.—We had travelled but two or three miles when we came to a group of boiling springs. I did not count them, but there can not be less than twenty, nearly all varying more or less in temperature. One of the springs I supposed to be twenty feet in diameter, of unfathomable depth and boiling like a pot. From the appearance of the ground around which is perfectly bare of vegetation, they sometimes overflow. They attract the attention of every passer-by, and this strange phenomenon of nature is only beheld with wonder and surprise.*

Madison Moorman, 1850

Ruby Lake, Nevada

Canyon—South Fork of Humboldt River, Nevada

Lichen—South Fork Canyon, Nevada

*Aug. 14th.—We made an early start, without breakfast, and when we had travelled a mile or two we entered a very rugged Kanyon of six or seven miles continuance. We crossed four or five times the, here, very rapid and deep little river, and sometimes, to avoid a crossing, we would leave the wagon track and risk a hazardous bridle way on the steep and rugged mountain side, from which an awkward step of our sure footed mules would have hurled us a hundred feet and launched us in the river foaming in the depths below. Several of our animals stuck fast in the miry banks and to extricate one of which hard pulling at ropes and deep wading into mud and water were necessary.—Ten miles travel brought us into the Old Road and a mile or two down we halted and had breakfast and dinner together.*

Madison Moorman, 1850

Canyon—South Fork of Humboldt River, Nevada

Lizard tracks, sand dunes—Humboldt Lake, Nevada

WHEN THAT EXCEPTIONAL journalist and artist, J. Goldsborough Bruff, came upon the headwaters of the Humboldt in 1849, he merely entered this brief historical notation in his journal to mark the occasion:

"SEPT. 3. . . . 6 a.m. we rolled on; over a good road, short rolling hills, and S. and S. W. course 10 a.m. entered a moist flat valley, trending round to the Westward, with springs, and a grassy and willowy rivulet;—one of the heads of the Humboldt—(This stream was first known by the name of Ogden's river,—so they say; afterwards called Mary's river, probably in honor of the Blessed Virgin; and continued by that name, till Col. Fremont re-christened it, in honor of Baron Humboldt. Some travellers adopt the last name, but it is generally called 'Mary's river.')"

This first meeting with the Humboldt was perhaps the only time that such a dispassionate comment would be made concerning the strange desert river that was to become the great psychological bugaboo of the California Trail. By the time the emigrant had reached the end of his two or three weeks of forced association with the Humboldt, he would undoubtedly be in a frame of mind to agree with the acerbic remarks of Elisha Perkins:

"Friday Sept. 7. . . . Here we see our last of the famous Humboldt & I must agree with the majority of the Emigrants in nicknaming it "Humbug River." The stream itself does not deserve the name of river being only a good sized creek, about like our Duck Creek only longer & running through a more level country. For the first two day's travel in its valley the grass is splendid, then the valley begins to narrow & feed to get poorer & less of it all the rest of its course, till for the last 80 miles except in special spots we could hardly get enough for our mules to eat, & water barely drinkable from saline & sulphurous impregnation & having a milky color. I think Baron Humboldt would feel but little honored by his name being affixed to a stream of so little pretension. . . ."

Certainly no other single geographical feature along the entire trek from the States caused the California-bound emigrant so much emotional anguish as the Humboldt River. It was the one stretch of the California Trail that

# The Humboldt River Route

Beetle on desert flower—Humboldt Sink, Nevada

107

every emigrant had to follow; it was *the* great common misery, the object of unanimous damnation. At either end of this section of trail the traveler at least had some choice as to route, but down the sluggish, meandering Humboldt, all were required to march together.

By any standards, the river was a curious affair. Franklin Langworthy put his finger on one of its curious features when he pointed out: "The Humboldt is a singular stream; I think the longest river in the world, of so diminutive a size. Its length is three or four hundred miles, and general width about fifty feet. From here, back to where we first saw it, the quantity of water seems about the same. It rather diminishes in size as it proceeds."

The emigrants, of course, were all used to the great rivers of the Atlantic seaboard or the Mississippi Valley, where a proper creek grew to a decent stream to a respectable river—gathering size and strength all the way along until it debouched into the ocean. That was the proper order of things from anything that they had ever known or experienced. This desert river was not only completely unfamiliar and thus suspect, but it was almost to be considered sinister in both mood and surroundings. Reuben Shaw sums it all up nicely when he cautions us:

"The reader should not imagine the Humboldt to be a rapid mountain stream, with its cool and limpid waters rushing down the rocks of steep inclines, with here and there beautiful cascades and shady pools under mountain evergreens, where the sun never intrudes and where the speckled trout loves to sport. While the water of such a stream is fit for the gods, that of the Humboldt is not good for man nor beast. With the exception of a short distance near its source, it has the least perceptible current. There is not a fish nor any other living thing to be found in its waters, and there is not timber enough in three hundred miles of its desolate valley to make a snuff-box, or sufficient vegetation along its banks to shade a rabbit, while its waters contain the alkali to make soap for a nation, and, after winding its sluggish way through a desert within a desert, it sinks, dis-

appears, and leaves inquisitive man to ask how, why, when and where."

And, yet, while the emigrant might have been frustrated and angered and even fearful of the Humboldt, he also knew that whether he liked it or not, he was utterly dependent upon it to bring him on to California. He was therefore put in that most unhappy position of having to depend on and give thanks for the very thing that he grew to loathe. Perhaps seldom in the history of human migration have so many been so beholden to that which was so loathsome. The ambivalence of the emotional experience was to bring flashes of color to even the most prosaic of diaries.

The region around the headwaters of the river was decent enough—good grass and clear, cool waters rippling over rocky streambeds—but then the Humboldt settled down to meander with an ever-lessening current and ever-increasing turbidity and alkalinity through long stretches of sandy desert, interrupted only at infrequent intervals by nearly impassable canyons through the mountains. This was a region of sage and rabbit bush, where the only things even approaching tree size were the shrub-like willows along the river banks. Between the region of natural meadows at the head of the river and the Great Meadows that were found where the river took its wide swing to the south just west of present-day Winnemucca, the general rule was that grass was patchy, of poor quality, often difficult to reach, and confined to the immediate area of the river. Often, grass was to be found only in low-lying areas of swamp, and the emigrants had to go out and cut it by hand to keep the stock from getting bogged down. It was only at one of the true marvels of the lower Humboldt, that stock-saving region known as the Great Meadows, that there was a plentitude of grass. There the prudent emigrant could rest for a few days and take full advantage of this last opportunity to recruit his animals.

But it wasn't only the general scarcity and poor quality of grass and water that caused the emigrant so much vexation. Sometimes the river snaked off into impassable canyons, and the trail had to swing away over waterless, sage-covered bluffs for considerable distances on what were known as dry *jornadas* before coming back to water. At other times, high water would force the wagons away from the river bottom and cause further tedious detours. Below the Great Meadows, the river cut a considerable canyon through the loose sediments of ancient lake beds, and it was most difficult to get the stock down and back up from feeding and watering.

And then there was the matter of the water itself. With every passing mile it deteriorated in quality and became less and less acceptable to both humans and animals alike. It became ever more tepid and salty and alkaline; the color went from chalky-white to yellowish-green to putrid brown as it seeped with fetid sluggishness into the cattail marshes and shallow, reed-filled waters of Humboldt Lake. From the lake, it oozed through a salt-encrusted channel into the alkali-whitened bed of the sink itself and then on around the point of the mountains to mingle with the equally evil-smelling fluids of the adjoining sink of the Carson River. The smell, the taste, and the sight all combined to make this part of the journey like something right out of purgatory.

The main trail itself followed mostly down the north side of the river until it reached the vicinity of Gravelly Ford above Beowawe. From that point, the emigrants pushed routes down both sides as they sought to find shortcuts and new areas of grass for their stock. The north bank was still the more popular route, but there was much crossing back and forth as each wagon or train of wagons tried to gain the advantage in time and forage over those ahead and behind.

From the vicinity of the Great Meadows on down to the sink, the trail along the south bank was sometimes referred to as being on "the Mormon side." It probably received this designation because the Mormon-opened Carson Pass Route lay in that southerly direction and there was also some movement of Mormons back to Salt Lake City from California along that side in 1849. It is also well known that the nature of feelings at the time usually caused Mormons to keep to themselves when traveling near or among the cursed gentiles (and vice versa), and that undoubtedly had something to do with them attempting to keep to a separate path away from the main body of emigrants. However, after 1849 there are no reports of Mormons along this section of the trail and these feelings of mutual suspicion and ill will were never enough at any time to prevent many non-Mormons from availing themselves of this alternate route along the south bank if they were heading for Carson Pass or if it was late in the season and all the grass had been eaten off along the main trail, as it often was in years of scant rainfall or heavy migration.

All in all, the toilsome 330 or so miles down this desert river were a never-to-be-forgotten experience. It was not so much that the emigrant was ever in any real danger of perishing for want of food or grass or water, but rather that the *potential* for such a disaster was always hovering at the edges of consciousness like a real but inarticulated threat. This persistent fear, combined with the tediousness of the march, the threatened depredations of the Diggers, and the unsettling strangeness of the terrain, made this section of the trail a psychological nightmare. Each emigrant—depending on the limits of his or her own temperament and moral convictions—either openly and loudly profaned the whole unhappy affair or assumed a role of quiet resignation, but surely none ever forgot it. It was a truly unique part of the great journey—this most necessary, if damnable, Humboldt.

North Fork of Humboldt River, Nevada

*The valley about the head waters of Mary's river is a most beautiful valley. You will see the Humboldt mountains not far distant on your left, covered with everlasting snows, while you are in the valley below, melting under the scorching rays of the sun.*

*Platt and Slater Guide,* 1852

Wells, Nevada

*Monday 20 Augᵗ ... This is I think one of the most detestable countries God ever made, to say nothing of its sterility and barrenness. The nights are so cold we cannot keep warm in bed, ice forms every night. this morning the water froze in a dish after daylight. While the middle of the day the sun pours down his beams, and the heat is as oppressive as at Sᵗ Louis.*

James F. Wilkins, 1849

Morning ice—Wells, Nevada

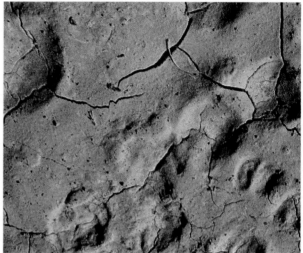

*SEPT. 11th... Forenoon's drive across a broad alkali desert; face of it glazed and cracked white earth, (had been, in wet season, mud) filling the road with an impallpable white powder....*

Alkali mud—Humboldt River, Nevada

*Fragments of agates, carnelians, chalcedony & semi-opal, and pieces of arrow-heads, formed of these stones, abundant. On the hill on our left I found many, and the large quartz rock and minute fragments around, with place of a fire near by each big stone, where the indians had spent some days manufacturing arrow-points.*

J. Goldsborough Bruff, 1849

Gravelly Ford—Beowawe, Nevada

Dust devils—Humboldt River, Nevada

*May 17.... The vallies are composed of find mud thrown from the bowels of the earth*
*in great Quantities mixed with Boiling water and when left exposed to the weather*
*for an unknown time the water being evaporated by the sun leaves this remarkable*
*fine clay which is soft and fine flour  whirlwinds and other strong currents of wind*
*carry large Quantitiees to a great hight resembling a white smoke which in times of*
*dry weather and strong winds completely obscures the light and resembles thin light fog.*

James Clyman, 1846

*Saturday Sept. 1. Another beautiful Indian summer hazy morning with its soft air, & deathlike stillness. How I have enjoyed such mornings at home, under the shade of some trees to lay & meditate & dream. But here it is nought but push on, push on, & ever must be astir.*

Elisha Perkins, 1849

Sunrise—Great (Lassen's) Meadows, Nevada

*Thousands of white birds, larger than swans, swam majestically on the calm and oily water of the lake. Their beaks were large & somewhat long. Their wings were tipped with a black line at the extremity of the pinions. Before they could rise on the wing, they were obliged to take a long run on the water.*

Jules Remy, 1855

Whistling swans—Humboldt Lake, Nevada

Humboldt Lake, Nevada

*July 13 I again set out eight miles from my place of encampment  I find the head of Humboldt Lake  this is a butiful lake ten miles long and six miles wide. The traveler should cut grass and take water eight miles before coming to the lake to last him across the desert—as little water as can be made use of from the lake for man or beast is advisable. This is the most god forsaken spot that the eye of man ever beheld  water poisen verry little grass, no wood and the scorching rais of the sun put a grate burthen on the travelers shoulders.*

Jay Green, 1852

Humboldt River—Great (Lassen's) Meadows, Nevada

In 1846 a route to southern Oregon was opened eastward from the Willamette Valley by the Applegate Party. This route crossed the northeastern corner of California below Goose Lake and then proceeded generally south and eastward to come into the main Humboldt River Trail at Great Meadows. In 1848, Peter Lassen, who traveled east in the spring from California, persuaded a group of emigrants to follow a new route to the Sacramento Valley and his rancho. His route followed the Applegate Route as far as Goose Lake and then cut south and west through mountainous plateau country that had not been previously scouted by him. After much hardship, the wagons succeeded in getting through. In 1849, this new trail was heavily used by emigrants and gold seekers who mistakenly thought it was a short-cut to the Great Valley.

This route led from Great Meadows on the bend of the Humboldt (soon to be known as Lassen's Meadows) to Lassen's Rancho on the Sacramento River, by way of Black Rock Desert, Fandango Pass, Pit River, Big Meadows–Feather River, and Deer Creek Ridge.

The Applegate portion of the trail left the Humboldt River at the Great Meadows (now Rye Patch Reservoir) and headed directly west across a sage flat to the base of the Antelope Mountains. Here the emigrants could get some small amounts of water at Antelope Springs (Willow Springs), but there was little or no grass for the stock, and the water was not sufficient for large trains.

The original Applegate route then led through a pass on the northwestern spur of Majuba Mountain (perhaps it should be named Applegate Pass), but very soon an alternate route opened up over Imlay Summit on a northeasterly spur, which was in a slightly more direct line with Rosebud Canyon and Rabbithole Springs. At Rabbithole there was again no grass, and water in the pit wells was scarce. From there the trail led directly down the sage-covered slopes to the alkali flats of Mud Lake (Black Rock Desert) and across them to the Great Boiling Springs at Black Rock Point itself. This was another grassless, waterless reach of twenty-five miles.

The trail then followed a northerly course

# The Applegate-Lassen Route

Autumn redbud leaves—California Foothills

along the western base of the beautiful Black Rock Range, moving from spring to spring past lofty Pahute Peak (where Peter Lassen was to meet his death some years later) to Mud Meadows and good grass and water at Lower Soldier Meadow. From here the trail turned west over very rocky ridges to the famous descent into High Rock Canyon and the spacious basin of High Rock Lake. The route through the Calico Mountains was along a natural avenue formed by High Rock Canyon and provided adequate water and feed.

The trail continued its northwesterly course to Emigrant Springs and Painted Point, then swung directly west across Long Valley, through Forty-nine Pass, and into Surprise Valley, from which the emigrants caught first sight of the vaunted "Sierra Nevada" (actually the Warner Range of the Cascade system). Here the route led across the valley, between Upper and Lower Alkali lakes, and turned abruptly north along the stream-watered slopes of the Warner Range to make the extremely hard, steep ascent to Fandango Pass.

From this hard-won summit it was possible for the emigrant to preview his route down Fandango Valley to Goose Lake, where the trail turned southward and skirted the shores of that very large and brackish body of water. At the southern point of Goose Lake, the Applegate Trail swung north and west toward Oregon, and the Lassen section began.

The California-bound emigrant now went south along the eastern edge of the canyon of the North Fork of the Pit River (a northern branch of the Sacramento), dropped into the canyon, passed Chimney Rocks, and turned west above Alturas into the open valley of the Pit River. There was now easy going through volcanic plateau country to a point just west of Canby, where the river entered another canyon. The trail followed right down this canyon with numerous difficult fordings and came out at the northern edge of Round Valley (Big Valley), where it struck the old trapper route to Oregon and turned directly south past Bieber to the southern tip of this extensive valley.

Here, the Pit again entered a canyon, which was this time impassable for wagons, and the emigrant had a choice of routes. One branch forded the Pit and cut across the very rocky point of the mountain, which was formed by a great northern bend in the river, reforded into Fall River Valley, and then turned south to climb via Beaver Creek and Willow Springs to rejoin the other trail just above Beaver Springs on Blacks Mountain. The other route (called the mountain route) struck directly southward up the stony mountainside to Clark Valley and the favorite camping place in Little Valley. Then it swung westerly around the point of Black's Ridge and climbed directly up the mountain to Beaver Springs and the point just beyond where the trails rejoined.

The reunited emigrants continued south around the western slopes of Blacks Mountain to Jelly Spring and then eastward to Patterson Flat, Dixie Springs, and Harvey Valley. From here they swung back westward to Grays Valley and then southeast to Pine Creek Valley and Feather and Mud lakes. (Within a few years, the section of Lassen's Trail from Grays Valley to Mud Lake was to coincide with a short section of Nobles' Trail, and thus one would find traffic moving along it in both a northerly and southerly direction at the same time. Within a short time, too, the easterly meander of the original trail to Dixie Springs was made needless by the opening of a route directly south from Blacks Mountain past Poison Lake to Grays Valley.)

From Feather or Mud Lake, the trail dropped south through Norvell Flat to Robbers Creek, Dry Creek, and the spring-fed lake at Clear Creek. It turned west from Clear Creek along the northern banks of the Hamilton Branch of the Feather River, forded Rock Creek, passed near Big Springs, swung over Almanor Peninsula, and reached the Feather River at beautiful and lush Big Meadows (now Lake Almanor).

The emigrants usually rested and recruited their animals at Big Meadows, then headed west again along Soldier Creek and through Deer Creek Pass to Deer Creek Meadows. This was the last possible place where they would find grass until they crawled out onto the rocky slopes of the Sacramento Valley, as the trail now climbed up and followed out the heavily forested, dry, hot ridge between Mill and Deer creeks. From the point where the Great Valley first opened out before the emigrants' eyes, it was a rough, hard ride over rocks and sun-scorched grass to the end of the trail under the great oaks at Lassen's Rancho at the mouth of Deer Creek on the Sacramento River.

This Applegate-Lassen Route had only one year of great usage—1849, the second year it was open. That year the rumor circulated among the emigrants and gold seekers at Great Meadows on the Humboldt that this was a new and shorter route to the Sacramento Valley, and before the season was over, it had been estimated that between one-third and one-half of all the California-bound travelers turned off that way.

It was not a bad route. There were some difficulties, to be sure: the treacherous ascent at Fandango Pass, the miserable crossing of Black Rock Desert (although it is doubtful that it was any more difficult than the desert cross-ings on either the Carson or Truckee River routes), the hard going through the Pit River Canyon into Big Valley, the rough trail out of Big Valley, and finally the dry drive along the Mill Creek Ridge. But generally the topog-raphy was open plateau country with easy gradients and adequate water and grass. If any-thing, this route was, mile for mile, easier than any of the previously opened routes; the real trouble was there were just *too many miles!*

Most of the emigrants left the Humboldt fully expecting to be in the California settle-ments in a week, and many, many weeks later they stumbled out into the Great Valley only to find that they had had to travel some 135 miles farther to get there, and they were *still* 70 miles from the town of Sacramento and the gold fields. Those seeking gold were infuriated to be still so far away from their destination, and those emigrants with families found themselves near starvation because of the unexpected ex-tra weeks of travel. Indeed, only a massive effort by both the settlers and the army kept many of the late-season travelers from being trapped and actually starving in the snows of early winter.

Added to this sense of anger and the feeling that they had been "had" was the additional factor that the Indians along the whole route from the Humboldt—and especially the Pit and Modoc tribes of northeastern California—had been openly and murderously hostile to this invasion of white men. They weren't con-tent just to sneak up at night, shoot a cow or two, and melt into the darkness again; they put many a settler into his grave, too.

No wonder there was much muttering about extracting some measure of retribution from Mr. Lassen, and small wonder that this route immediately received an evil reputation among the emigrants. Sizable numbers continued to use the Applegate section of it in order to go on to Oregon, but the Lassen section was largely abandoned as its reputation was made known by those who had suffered on it. To many it continued to be known derisively as Green-horn's Cutoff, or Lassen's Horn Route, or even more cruelly, Lassen's Death Horn Route.

The subsequent discovery of gold in the northern part of the state gave the route some further use, but continuing and expanding In-dian troubles and the subsequent opening of shorter, easier routes into the northern Sacra-mento Valley combined to keep it a little-used alternative.

Great (Lassen's) Meadows, Nevada

*August 10. Reports began to reach us of hard roads ahead; that there was no grass
at the Sink, or place where the river disappears in the sands of the desert, and from
that place a desert of sand, with water but once in forty-five miles, had to be crossed.
In our worn-out condition this looked discouraging, and it was with a kind of dread
that we looked to the passage of that sandy plain. At the same time an indefinite tale
was circulated among the emigrants, that a new road had been discovered, by which
the Sacramento might be reached in a shorter distance, avoiding altogether the
dreaded desert; and that there was plenty of grass and water on the route. It was said,
too, that on this route the Sierra Nevada Mountains could be crossed with but little
difficulty, while on the other it was a work of great labor and some risk....*

*August 15. Learning that the northern road turned off about three miles below us,
we moved down, and, turning our cattle out, held a consultation with regard to our
main course. A man on horseback reported that he had gone thirty miles out on the
route; that in ten miles there was grass, in twelve grass and water, and in twenty,
grass and water in abundance; and on reaching Rabbit Springs, a distance of thirty-
five miles, all difficulty would be ended. Others said that for thirty-five miles there
was neither grass nor water; that the road did not go to California at all, but to
Oregon, and that the Indians were troublesome and bad. Some said that only half a
dozen trains had gone that way; that they were led by McGee, a man who had lived
in California, and was well acquainted with the country, and who expected to find
a route over the mountains.*

 *Colonel Kinkead was anxious to take this route, but his family becoming alarmed on
hearing of the hostility of the Indians, and the doubts and perplexities of going
through an unknown, mountainous country, finally induced the Colonel to abandon
the idea, and keep on the old beaten track—a measure which was most happy for
him, and proved that women's fears are at least sometimes well grounded. It was
decided, finally, that we would go the northern route, although some of our company
had misgivings. The younger portion being fond of adventure, were loud in
favor of the road.*

Alonzo Delano, 1849

Desert crossing to Antelope Springs, Nevada

*SEP. 19.... A broad and perfectly level semi-circular area, very dusty, sweeps around the bend—and the two trails, or roads, are broad and as well beaten as any travelled thoroughfare can be. On the right, about a hundred yds. from the Bend, the Desert route branches off, and in the forks of the road, I observed a red painted barrel standing.—I rode up, to examine it.—It was a nice new barrel, about the size of a whisky-barrel, iron hoops, and a square hole cut in the head; and neatly painted in black block letters, upon it, "POST OFFICE". On looking in, I found it half-full of letters, notes, notices, &c.— Near this was a stick and bill-board, also filled with notices.—These were chiefly directed to emigrants in the rear, hurrying them along, giving information about route, telling who had taken this or the southern route, &c. By these I ascertained that few had taken the Southern road.*

J. Goldsborough Bruff, 1849

Antelope Springs, Nevada

*We continued to travel very rapidly all day over a desert that appeared to be boundless,
. . . the earth appeared to be as destitute of moisture, as if a drop of rain or dew
had never fallen upon it from the brazen heavens above. . . . There being neither water
nor grass for our poor, toil-worn cattle, they were carefully guarded through the
night. I had gone forward in the morning, and found, within about three-fourths of a
mile of our encampment, and far up the side of the mountain, a very small vein of
water, that moistened the ground a few yards around. I removed a considerable
quantity of earth with my spade, so as to make a little reservoir. Into this the water
very slowly collected, and enough was obtained for tea; and from it, a few of the
cattle received, perhaps half a pint of water apiece.*

J. Quinn Thornton, 1846

Rabbithole Springs, Nevada

*After traveling about fifteen miles we began to discover dim rabbit trails running
in the same direction in which we were traveling. As we advanced the trails became
more plain, and there were others constantly coming in, all pointing in the general
direction toward a ledge of granite boulders which we could see before us.
Approaching the ledge, ... we could see a green mound where all the trails seemed to
enter, and on examining the place closely we found a small hole in the top of the
mound, in which a little puddle of water stood within a few inches of the surface....
Digging down in the clay we made a basin large enough to hold several gallons and
by dark we had quite a supply of good pure water.... Great numbers of rabbits came
around us and we killed all we wanted of them. This is the place always since
known as the Rabbit Hole Springs.*

Lindsay Applegate, 1846

*August 16.... The day was excessively warm.... After ascending a little elevation,
the glad shout was raised, "I see where the spring is!" Several wagons had stopped
in the road, and a knot of men were gathered around a particular spot, which
marked the place of the glorious element, and with parched tongues we went up.
Judge of our disappointment, when we found the promised springs to be only three
or four wells sunk in the ground, into which the water percolated in a volume about
the size of a straw, and each hole occupied by a man dipping it up with a pint cup,
as it slowly filled a little cavity in the ground. Each man was taking his turn to drink,
and we had ample time to get cool before our turn came to taste the muddy water;
and as to getting a supply for our cattle, it was out of the question. Beyond us,
far as we could see, was a barren waste, without a blade of grass or a drop of
water for thirty miles at least.*

Alonzo Delano, 1849

Rosebud Canyon, Nevada

Mud Lake and Black Rock Point, Nevada

*August 17. . . . We found this to be an oasis in the desert. . . . The desert and the
mountain were all the eye could view beyond the little patch of grass, and the naked
salt plain which we had crossed, proved to be the dry bed of Mud Lake. After the
snows melt on the mountains, and the spring rains come on, the plain is a reservoir
for the waters, making an extensive lake, which the hot sun of a long summer
evaporates, leaving its bed dry and bare. Far to the south was another gorge, bounded
on the east by a light gray granite mountain, which led to Pyramid Lake, and was
the route taken by Fremont to California, on his return from Oregon. Beyond
Black Rock Mountain were other peaks, which united with a chain north of us, and
along the base of which we were to travel in a westerly course.*

Alonzo Delano, 1849

Mud Lake, Nevada

131

Black Rock Point, Nevada

*Just as the sun was sinking, we resumed our journey, and after descending a little hill we entered a country more forbidding and repulsive than even that I have described. There we occasionally saw a stray and solitary bush of artemisia. It was a country which had nothing of a redeeming character. Nothing presented itself to the eye, but a broad expanse of a uniform dead level plain, which conveyed to the mind the idea that it had been the muddy and sandy bottom of a former lake; and, that after the water had suddenly sunk through the fissures, leaving the bottom in a state of muddy fusion, streams of gas had broken out in ten thousand places, and had thrown up sand and mud; so as to form cones, rising from a common plane, and ranging from three to twenty feet in height. It seemed to be the River of Death dried up, and having its muddy bottom jetted into cones by the force of the fires of perdition.*

J. Quinn Thornton, 1846

132

*SEP T. 21. . . . When we reached the white plain, I found that it was cover'd with a smooth white encrustation, probably alkaline. A very beautiful Mirage in the S.S.W. on this plain, at base of some mountains. In which appeared a long lagoon of light blue water, bordered with tall trees, small islands and their reflection in its delightful looking bosom. One of my men asked me if it was possible that that apparent lake was not water?—I explained it, and informed him that not only was it such a plain as we here stoon [stood] on, but that those pretty cedar-looking trees were only dusty dwarf sage bushes; and the whole landscape was aerial except the outline of the mountains. He was astonished, and an uninformed person might well be. Oxen had stampeded for it, hoping to quench their burning thirst, and left their swelled-up carcasses over the plain in that direction, as far as we could descern them.*

J. Goldsborough Bruff, 1849

Black Rock from across Mud Lake Desert, Nevada

Grass and reeds—Black Rock Spring, Nevada

Black Rock Spring, Nevada

*SEPT. 22. . . . This is a very remarkable place.—All volcanic, and in combustion no
extraordinary depth below ground. Marshes and plains of poor grass: Streams, or
spring rivulets of saline, sulphur, & warm water. The Great Boiling Spring,
is like all others I have seen,—a raised circular tumola, about 30 feet diameter on top,
basin shap'd within, dark bubbling water, overflowing one edge, and received into
a circular reservoùr, dug some yards lower down, and from that into a 3d reservoùr,
in which last it is cool enough to use for ordinary purposes.—The Spring is
too hot to put your hand in, and the 1st reservoùr is quite warm. Looking into the
great basin I could see, apparently about 4 ft from the surface, a black hole,
about the size of my head.*

J. Goldsborough Bruff, 1849

*August 18. The water in the springs
was clear and deep, and hot enough
to boil bacon. We boiled our coffee by
setting the coffee-pot in the water.
Near them was one of lukewarm
water, another of magnesia, and one
that was quite cold. All these were
within the space of a quarter of
an acre.*

Alonzo Delano, 1849

Double Hot Springs, Nevada

Double Hot Springs, Nevada

Frēmont's Castle—Black Rock Desert, Nevada

*Sept. 23.... From our position at noon across the valley to the N. by W. was a
very remarkable resemblance of a castle or fortress, of a white substance, (probably
clay), in the face of a brownish hill, resting on a shelf of the rock, about ⅓ from
the plain; This I sketch'd, and named it Fremont's Castle....*

*SEP. 25.... On right of the road—mere trail,—on a small elevation, surrounded by
marsh, is a grave, the board enscribed thus:—*

*"C. H. Bintly,
from Yorkshire, England
Died Sep. 9th, 1849,
Aged 43 years."*

*Relics of camps and discarded effects, carcases, &c. around.*

*After nooning we pushed on,—over a badly diversified and crooked a trail as
could be found. In fact, to avoid the marshes, there were many trails, and we adopted
that most travelled. About a mile of alternate marsh and level baked earth; then
over volcanic powder and surfaces—generally level, but McAdamiz'd with crude
sharp volcanic fragments, resembling broken cast iron, mixed with scoriae
from a furnace exceedingly bad for the animal's feet, and racking to vehicles,
and annoying to pedestrians....*

Black Rock Range, Nevada

*The vale where we were camped, last night was covered with volcanic ashes, and
sprinkled with fragmentary basaltes, tufa, pumice, lava,—red, yellow, and grey,
(similar specimens, from Eatna and Vesuvius, in my cabinet, Washington City.)
Pretty white calcedony, and obsidian arrow heads numerous; found here, among the
willows, near the brook, decayed remains of an indian-lodge, in which was a
wolf's scull, and several flint and obsidian arrow heads. . . .*

J. Goldsborough Bruff, 1849

Volcanic debris—Black Rock Desert, Nevada

139

Dust devil—Upper Mud Lake, Nevada

Desert rill—Mud Lake Meadows, Nevada

*At last we made a devious and steep sand descent, among large sage and grease-wood bushes, into a narrow bottom, in which is a brook running through a deep and very rocky gulch, passing through a sort of cañon below into Mud Lake. Near the stream on its western side, was a small dug tank of good cool water, several pools of good water, and a marsh. It was dusk when we reached this, and on a pretty level grassy spot, surrounded by trees and bushes, in this deep narrow vale, stood a tent, a wagon and cart, and a couple of rush-bottom'd chairs, by the dying embers of a fire, around which were some cooking utensils, &c—The folks, (a family with them) were in the tent and wagon asleep. Their cattle were grazing about ¼ mile off, and the tinkling of the cow-bell sounded very domestic. . . .*

Entrance to High Rock Canyon, Nevada

*While ascending this elevation, I had a fine view around, but the harsh angularly ruptured country close on my right, attracted my particular attention, and attracted a sketch. All volcanic. The road terminated, as it were, at the edge of the very apex of this hill, and from a big rock on the left of trail, at crest, I looked down, and for a while thought it must be "the jumping-off place"! . . . Here, down this very steep descent, must our wagons roll! (I observed to friend Barker, that I thought is a very de scent road.) Well, it was only about 200 yards, very deep sand, and loose stones. we double locked the wheels, and teamsters and assistants carefully lead the mules, and one after the other, slowly, and successfully, was the entire train taken down on the plateau below. On looking back; it seemed amazing that wagons and teams could descend in safety.—100 yards S. out from the descending road, the cliff formed an acute angle, and side of the yawning mouth of a cañon, an immense narrow rugged chasm, rent in the hills. The declivity, and its base, retained vestages of unfortunate travelling, in the shape of broken wagons, wheels, hubs, tires, axles, &c and 3 dead oxen.*

J. Goldsborough Bruff, 1849

First view of the ''Sierra'' (Warner Mountains)—Surprise Valley, California

*August 26. The Sierra Nevada—the snowy mountain so long wished for, and yet so long dreaded! We were at its base, soon to commence its ascent. In a day or two we were to leave the barren sands of the desert for a region of mountains and hills, where perhaps the means of sustaining life might not be found; where our wagons might be dashed to atoms by falling from precipices. A thousand vague and undefined difficulties were present to our imaginations; yet all felt strong for the work, feeling that it was our last.*

Alonzo Delano, 1849

*The little valley was fringed with mountain mahogany trees, giving it quite a picturesque appearance. This shrub, which is peculiar to the rocky highlands, is from fifteen to twenty feet high and in form something like a cherry tree, so that a grove of mountain mahogany strikingly resembles a cherry orchard.*

Lindsay Applegate, 1846

Wild fruit—Fandango Pass, California

*OCT. 3ᵈ . . . Reached the foot of the big hill,—a long and smooth sand drag, pretty steep ascent.— 10 dead oxen marked the trail. Across the road about midway up this hill, lay an ox on his knees,—dying, and covered with old gum coat, by his compassionate owner; but it was unavailing,—the dust was suffocating, and the animals and wheels went over him, in the haste and trouble of the steep ascent. The first wagon of my train, which reach'd the top of the Pass, displayed the Stars and stripes, to encourage those in the rear. Found many ox-wagons on the flat top of the Pass. . . .*

*While on top of the Pass, looking down the Eⁿ side, at the bustle, and directing the ascent, I was amused.*

*I thought the infirm ox in the road below, occupied rather an unenviable position.— In the centre of a very broad, sandy, and dusty road, men urging their heavy oxtrains up the steep hill, with lashes, imprecations, & shouts, some riding up on horses & mules, and clouds of blinding dust & sand flying. There rode up, an old man, on a jaded horse; a matress covered the horse, the sick man astride and laying over on his breast, with a coverlid thrown over him, and a corner trailing in the dust, he looked pale and haggard; had his arms around the neck of the old horse. He was afflicted with the flux and scurvy. Another unfortunate followed him, on a mule, enveloped in a blue blanket, and barely able to retain his seat; he had the fever and ague. Some small boys, not over 10 years of age, were leading jaded animals up. Women were seen, with the trains, occupied at chocking the wheels, while the oxen were allowed to blow, on the ascent. A man had a baby in his arms, and in midst of the thick dust, was urging up his team. Some wagons had as many as 12 yoke of oxen in them. One wagon, with women and children in it, when near the summit, became uncoupled, and down hill it ran,—stern-foremost, with great rapidity.—The women and children screamed, men shouted, and with all the rest of the fuss, there was a great clamor. A dead ox, a short distance in front of a heavy team, and men by them, brought up the backing out vehicle, most luckily without damage to any one.*

J. Goldsborough Bruff, 1849

Upper Alkali Lake from Fandango Pass, California

Fandango Valley and Goose Lake, California

*August 31. The road led to a table plain above the valley, over Magnesia Hill, and then turned nearly west into the valley again, in about a mile. From the brow of the hill we had a charming prospect. The great valley extended many miles before us, and at the limit of vision, perhaps eighty miles distant, a high and apparently isolated snowy peak lifted its head to the clouds, like a beacon to travelers on their arduous journey, and the clear water of the Pitt was sparkling in the morning sun, as it wound its way, fringed with willows, through the grassy plain. The high, snow-capped butte was Mount Shasta; and though it appeared to us to be on a plain at the extremity of the valley, it was in fact surrounded by a broken and mountainous country, far from the course of the river. We crossed the river twice during the day by easy and safe fords, and found the volume of water increasing every hour.*

*We were overtaken at our noon halt by three packers, who told us that the emigration had again turned upon this road, in consequence of the failure of grass on the old road; that there was much suffering on the desert, and that the Indians were excessively bold and troublesome. If there was much selfishness shown on the road, there were occasional cases of genuine benevolence. They told us of one family, in which there were several small children whose cattle had all become exhausted, and had given out entirely. They were thus left destitute and helpless on the desert plain, without the possibility of moving. A company of young men came along, who were touched with compassion at their deplorable condition, and immediately gave up their own team to the distressed family, and traveled on foot themselves.*

Alonzo Delano, 1849

Mount Shasta (west of trail), California

Goose Lake, California and Oregon

*August 27. Once arrived at the summit, the view of mountain scenery is grand and beautiful. Below, on the west, at the distance of a mile, is a broad, green and grassy valley, abounding in springs. The valley is enclosed by high, pine-covered mountains, which seem to kiss the clouds; and at the distance of ten miles, at the extremity of the valley, is seen the broad, beautiful, blue water of Goose Lake, adding a charming variety to the scene. Turning to the east, and looking beyond the pines already passed, the dry basin of the lake, with its gray bed, seems to lay at our feet, surrounded by barren hills, which extent in a broken and irregular manner as far as the eye can see, and on each side the rocks and cliffs stand out in bold relief—the portals of the huge gate by which we enter the golden region of California.*

Alonzo Delano, 1849

Feather Lake, California

In 1820 a Spanish exploring expedition passed up the valley, headed by Captain
Louis A Arguello. By this party the name Rio de las Plumas, or Feather river,
was bestowed upon the stream, because of the great numbers of feathers of wild fowl
floating on its bosom. . . .

The water of Feather river, ½ mile below, as clear as crystal, bottom small pebbles,
and beautiful plants and long choralline looking grass in it, adhering to the flat
rocks.—Numerous fish swiming about as leasurely as gold fish in a vase. . . .

Women in groups, sitting by their wagons, children playing about, in the grass.
Mowers busy cutting hay, others tinkering on wagons, clothes drying on the green
grass; stately pines and furs, with their dark green foliage and bright brown trunks,
the broad grassy bottom—every shade of green and yellow, the pale green willows
marking the course of the stream and its branches; The tall mountains on the
opposite side, clothed with dark timber to their summits; the tents, wagons, &c.
make a beautiful and animated scene.

J. Goldsborough Bruff, 1849

Mountain Meadows (Lake Almanor), California

Sacramento Valley, California

*August 24. . . . Yet the imagined difficulties were without foundation. Instead of losing our wagons, and packing our cattle; or, as some suggested, as a last resort for the weary, mounting astride of an old ox, and thus making our debut into the valley of the land of gold—we were unable to add a single page of remarkable adventure across the mountains more dangerous than we had already encountered.*

Alonzo Delano, 1849

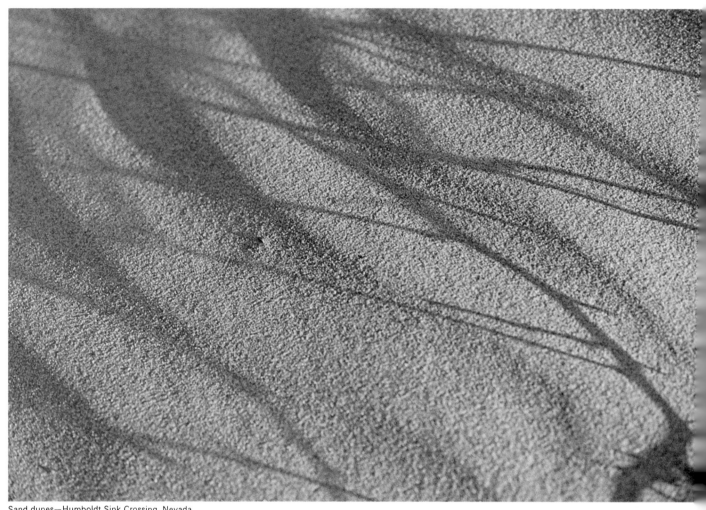

Sand dunes—Humboldt Sink Crossing, Nevada

THE PORTION OF THIS TRAIL through the Sierra Nevada was opened eastward in 1848 by a wagon train of Mormons (part of the California Mormon Battalion of the war with Mexico) returning to Salt Lake City. Their route on the eastern side of the Sierra ran north to the Truckee River to join into the Stevens-Donner Route where it came off the Forty-Mile Desert. In late 1848, a wagon train, coming from the States and captained by Joseph Chiles, dropped south and west from the Humboldt Sink to the Carson River and followed a route up the lower Carson River to come into the Carson Pass Trail opened earlier in the season by the Mormons.

This route ran from the Humboldt Sink to Hangtown (Placerville) and Sutter's Fort by way of the Carson River. It left the sink almost due south around the point of the West Humboldt Mountains, crossed the alkali flats, hummocks, and heavy sands bordering the western edge of the Carson Sink, and came to the Carson River at Ragtown, just to the south and west of Soda Lake. The main trail then proceeded up the north side of the Carson River for a way and then veered away from the meandering river for several short stretches and one twenty-six mile desert jornada before returning to the river near Dayton. From Dayton (Gold Canyon) it went twelve miles over the mountain spur to water in Eagle Valley (Carson City). Another good day of travel brought the emigrant to Mormon Station (Genoa) or just beyond to Walley's Hot Springs at the base of the Sierra, in the lush and beautiful Carson River Valley.

The next obstacle was the short but very difficult ascent of the canyon of the West Carson River to Hope Valley and an easy road to the base of the first summit of the Sierra at Red Lake. Here the trail made an almost perpendicular climb to the crest at Carson Pass and dropped down through heavily wooded, boulder-strewn country to the beautiful valley of Twin Lakes (Caple's Lake). The next day's journey was to the top of the second crest (9,500 feet—the highest altitude to be reached on any of the trails over the Sierra) on the volcanic spur above Silver Lake. Then the route led along the ridge to Corral Flat.

# The Mormon-Carson Route

Camus flower—Hope Valley, California

From Corral Flat it dropped off the ridge to Leek Springs and a fork in the trail. The northern branch went down the dividing ridge between Alder Creek and Camp Creek to a point just before Stump Springs, where it dropped steeply to water on Camp Creek; finally it followed down Stonebreaker Creek to Slys Park Creek and branched here for Placerville or Weber Creek.

The southern branch cut rather erratically southwest from Leek Springs along and across the ridges of the watershed of the Cosumnes River to Volcano. From any of these foothill gold regions there were trails down into the Central Valley and Sacramento (Sutter's Fort). The road from Hangtown (Placerville) went over the hill to Weber Creek and then to Diamond Springs, Mud Springs, Shingle Springs, White Rock Springs, and finally, Sacramento.

In 1852, the Johnson's Pass Cutoff was opened over Echo Summit just south of Lake Tahoe. It could be approached either by a route that climbed to Lake Tahoe from Eagle Valley (Carson City) and then went south around the lake to Meyers, which was just below the Pass, or by a route that came over Luther Pass from Hope Valley (the Pony Express Route of the early sixties). This trail then dropped down to Strawberry and more or less followed the same route as today's U.S. Highway 50 down to Placerville. This cutoff was shorter and crossed the Sierra at a much lower altitude than the Carson Route, but it was probably harder going and didn't compete seriously with the original route until the trails were improved to roads.

There was also another much used wagon trail which branched off of the original Mormon-Carson route in Hope Valley. This trail climbed up Faith and Charity valleys to pass over the Sierra crest into the Deer Creek drainage and then dropped down the ridges above the North Fork of the Stanislaus River to pass by the Calaveras Big Tree Groves. This route had considerable wagon travel in the 1850s and 1860s, and completely replaced the tortuous Sonora Route as the main wagon trail into the southern mines surrounding Sonora, Columbia and Murphys.

The Mormon-Carson Pass Route had its share of very difficult sections—the awful Forty Mile Desert crossing from the Humboldt Sink to the Carson River (the Truckee Route at least had water halfway across at the Boiling Springs—this Carson Route was dry the entire distance), the treacherous climb up the canyon of the West Carson to Hope Valley, the almost perpendicular climb above Red Lake to the first summit, and the generally hard pulling to the second summit. These were all decidedly negative factors.

But as a route it also had much to recommend it. When the mileage was added up, it was almost as direct a route to Sutter's Fort and Sacramento as the Stevens-Donner Route, and after gold was discovered, it had the great advantage of coming out right in the center of the early diggings. Perhaps above all, it had the reputation of being, overall, the easiest route. Since the Mormons had opened the route by following *eastward* up the coalescing ridges from their lowest points in the west, they had been able to pick out a relatively direct and easy wagon route while any trailblazers *from* the east could only start down a ridge and hope that it wouldn't end abruptly in a cliff or impossible canyon. This was a tremendous tactical advantage for the Mormons. And, to be quite honest, there was a tremendous element of luck involved in the opening of this route. The Mormons' course just happened to bring them through the backbone of the Sierra at that position that gave easiest access to the desert of Nevada.

The word soon spread among the emigrants that this was the best route to follow, and the records establish that it was soon the most popular trail into California, as it was to remain until improved roads came along and traffic was diverted elsewhere.

Along this route, too, there has been some unjustness in the naming of topographical features, although in this case there is considerably more justification than in the Stevens-Donner situation. Kit Carson did pass through this region with the Frémont exploring party of 1844 and even carved his name in a tree at the pass named for him. However, the only names to be retained from the Mormon opening are Slys Park, Hope Valley, and Tragedy Springs, where three of their number were mysteriously murdered, supposedly by Indians. One suspects that as far as the California-bound emigrants were concerned, this one unfortunate episode was as much commemoration as these self-styled Children of the New Zion could rightly expect; but nevertheless, the credit for the opening of this most important crossing of the Sierra was theirs.

Rainbow—Sierra Crest, California

Hummocks—Humboldt Sink, Nevada

*Sunday, July 15th.—A march of five hours brought us to the vicinity of the Sink of Humboldt River, at about nine o'clock; and continuing over a well beaten sandy trail until noon, we encamped on the edge of the Great Desert. Of late the region through which we journey had been growing more and more desolate; but here was reached what might be aptly termed "the valley of the shadow of death," and over its portals might be inscribed:*

*"Who enters here, leaves hope behind."*

*Towards the south—for in that direction the road bent, was a vast solitude covered with loose sand, which the wind heaped in hillocks, like waves of the sea. Scarce any vegetation existed; at long intervals might be seen a stalk of sage or greasewood, gnarled, blackened, and looking as if well nigh exhausted in its hard struggle for life. . . . Where we encamped, we found it necessary to dig wells for water. These wells, about four feet in diameter and of a trifle less depth, furnished an abundant supply of water, but intensely brackish, bitter with salt and sulphur. Some mules, and men also refused to drink of it; but, with nothing else to quench the thirst, we were painfully conscious that all would eventually use it, before better could be found.*

Wm. G. Johnston, 1849

Western edge of Carson Sink, Nevada

*August 5, 1850: Imagine to yourself a vast plain of sand and clay; . . . the stinted sage, the salt lakes, cheating the thirsty traveler into the belief that water is near; yes, water it is, but poison to the living thing that stops to drink. . . . Burning wagons render still more hideous the solemn march; dead horses line the road, and living ones may be constantly seen, lapping and rolling the empty water casks (which have been cast away) for a drop of water to quench their burning thirst, or standing with drooping heads, waiting for death to relieve them of their tortures, or lying on the sand half buried, unable to rise, yet still trying. The sand hills are reached; then comes a scene of confusion and dismay. Animal after animal drops down. Wagon afer wagon is stopped, the strongest animals are taken out of the harness; the most important effects are taken out of the wagon and placed on their backs and all hurry away, leaving behind wagons, property and animals that, too weak to travel, lie and broil in the sun. . . . The owners hurry on with but one object in view, that of reaching the Carson River before the boiling sun shall reduce them to the same condition. . . . The desert! You must see it and feel it in an August day, when legions have crossed it before you, to realize it in all its horrors. But heaven save you from the experience.*

E. S. Ingalls, 1850            159

Soda Lake, Nevada

*August 2d. . . . Our water being gone, we threw away our casks, tents, buffalo robes, and many other things, to lighten our load; we toiled on through the sand and heat, until we got within five miles of Pilot [Carson] river; here we understood there was a spring of good water, by the side of a small lake of salt water, on the top of a hill, . . . so we took our horses out of the harness and led them to the spring, which we easily found. On getting to the top of the hill, a small lake ushers itself into view, five or six hundred feet below you. A rather steep descent took us to the bottom, down which we succeeded in getting our horses; here, immediately at the bottom is one of the most beautiful springs I have ever seen, of most excellent water. Oh! how sweet and delicious is a draught of good cold water when you are suffering with burning thirst.*

J. S. Shepherd (undated)

Evening primrose—Soda Lake, Nevada

160

First view of Sierra Nevada—Carson River, Nevada

*From the summit of the rise we got the first good and distinct view of the Great Sierra Nevada range, stretching beyond the scope of vision, north and south, with pointed snow-capped peaks between us and the land of promise, reminding me of days gone by, the garden walls capped with glass to prevent naughty boys from stealing the rich fruit beyond them; but greedy urchins climbed the garden walls, and plucked the fruit, and avaricious men scaled the glaciered ridges of the mountain, and were gathering the treasure that nature enclosed so jealously.*

William Kelly, 1849

*You have now reached the north-east end of what is called* Carson Valley—*the largest fertile spot found on the route since leaving the head-waters of Mary's river. Along this valley you will find good grass. A small settlement was commenced in this valley, in the summer of 1851. The valley is about 30 miles long. . . . We would advise all to stop in this valley and recruit their teams before crossing the Nevada mountains.*

*Platt and Slater Guide, 1852*

Sunrise—Carson Valley, Nevada

Slough pond—Carson Valley, Nevada

*Sat., August 10—Took the trail this morning in good time. Have had good roads, by the side of a broad valley covered with a most luxuriant growth of fine grass. The hills or mountains very high and peaks tipped with snow. Their sides covered with pine timber of a large growth. I thought this one of the most beautiful sights I ever saw. We have travelled hundreds and hundreds of miles, and seen but little timber larger than the privet bushes in our garden at home. This change was pleasing indeed.*

George Read, 1850

Cottonwoods—Carson River, Nevada

Peaks of the Sierra—Mormon Station (Genoa), Nevada

Hot Springs (Walley's), Nevada

*Sunday Sep* 23 *Again it happens for the third time consecutively that we are making hay on the Sunday. Well the Lord will forgive us, I hope. this time we are making it (and I hope it is the last) to carry us thro the dreaded Kanyon. . . . Yesterday we passed boiling springs. the hot water gushed up from holes in the ground in several different places, tho' not actually boiling was so hot I could not hold my hand in. they ran into a little brook or slough forming a fine hot bath—*

James F. Wilkins, 1849

Grasses—Hot Springs, Nevada

Entrance to Carson Canyon, California

*On the 17th of October we reached the head of Carson Valley, and, just after noon, entered the great cañon. Here the road soon became so rough and steep as to make it very difficult for me to hold Mary and keep my seat. The men had hard work to drive the cattle and mules over the boulders at the frequent crossings of the stream, and in between the great masses of rock where the trail sometimes almost disappeared. As the cañon narrowed, the rocky walls towered nearly perpendicular, hundreds of feet; and seemed in some places almost to meet above our heads. At some of the crossings it was well nigh impossible to keep the trail, so innumerable were the boulders; and the scraggy bushes so hid the coming-out place. The days were shortening fast, and, in this deep gulch, darkness began to come on early. The animals became more and more restive with the roughness of the way, and it was hard work to keep them from rushing into a narrow ravine that occasionally opened, or up one of the steep trails which appeared now and then, suggesting unpleasant ideas of Indians and wild beasts. If our animals got many steps away we could not find them in the dusk.*

Sarah Royce, 1849

Carson Canyon, California

*Tuesday Sep'' 25. . . . He must have had a bold heart and a daring spirit, that first*
*conceived the idea of the possibility of wagons travelling thro' this mountain pass.*
*Imagine a mountain 6 miles thro' at its base cleft in twain, like an immense crack*
*and all the loose rocks and debris thrown together at the bottom, thro' which flows or*
*rather leaks a mountain stream, with here and there patches of scanty soil, bearing*
*loftey pines 4 and 5 ft in diameter amongst these rocks, and sometimes up steep hills*
*loaded wagons had to pass in places where loose cattle could hardly keep their feet.*
*the great difficulty was in steep places and short turns, where only one or two yoke*
*could pull at a time. every man had to put his shoulder to the wheel. here was the*
*place where light loads and strong wheels where [were] appreciated. the way all*
*along was strewn with broken wagons. the wheels had in some places to drop as*
*much as 3 or 4 ft onto solid rock. A pretty severe test to try the strength of a wheel.*
*But we got through safely, and congratulated ourselves so much that we took a*
*"horn" on the strength of it.*

James F. Wilkins, 1849

West Carson River, Carson Canyon, California

Upper Carson Canyon, California

*Aug. 4th. . . . The principal obstructions
that interposed themselves to our march was
the large piles of granit that had broken off
the walls of the Mountains which stood on
either side thousands of feet above us—and
over hanging us as it ware—and rolled
down into the gorge, forming piles from 1 to
300 feet high. These we were compelled to
find our way through by circuitous routs and
winding ways, Ascending and descending
over steep cragy cliffs and precipices. We
were compelled to force our wagons over,
around, and through, many of these places
by manuel labour and turnes being too short
to be made with the team hitched on. But
by a heard and loborious deys work, to our
selves and animals we succeeded in getting
through by 5 O'clock P.M. At the top of
which, we found a handsome vally of
grass [Hope Valley], Where we encamped
for the night.*

James Pritchard, 1849

Entrance to Hope Valley, California

*October 13th.—Sunday. . . . The road level for two miles, when we suddenly and*
*unexpectedly emerged from the cañon into a mountain valley. . . . Around the*
*landscape are dispersed clumps of pine and aspen trees, interspersed with many*
*large heaps of loose, granitic rocks. Through this lonely vale, the Carson river winds*
*its way, but is here diminished to the size of a small brook, with gentle curves,*
*rolling over the beds of pebbles. I think this valley must be six or seven thousand feet*
*above the level of the sea, as snow lies through the year at a little higher elevation.*
*Innumerable summits of rough, jagged, and snow-capped mountains, surround*
*the valley on all sides.*

Franklin Langworthy, 1850

Meadow wildflowers—Hope Valley, California

*Friday, September 26th—There are some of the most beautiful little valleys in these mountains, they are covered with bright, fresh looking flowers, the larkspur, bluebell, honeysuckle, and red flowers such as grow in Iowa and Illinois, they look as if it was spring.*

Jane Gould, 1862

Alpine primroses—Hope Valley, California

Mimulus—Second Summit, Carson Route, California

Yellow columbine—Charity Valley, California

Penstemon—Second Summit, Carson Route, California

Paint brush—Second Summit, Carson Route, California

Sedum—Second Summit, Carson Route, California

View toward Second Summit—Carson Route, California

*Friday morng 28th . . . Yesterday [September 27] we did not get of[f] till 9 O'clock, it being thought advisable to feed our oxen well before we started, as we had the second summit to ascend. it is I believe higher that the first, tho' the road is not so rocky, and fewer short turns on it. we doubled teams only for a mile or two, and reached the top. . . . here on the very summit of the back bone of the American continent, (and the backbone of the Elephant as the emigrants call it) we were favoured with a storm of hail rain and sleet. . . . to add to our difficulties the lady in our company was taken with the pangs of labour, and we had to descend as quickly as possible over a most rocky road, to the first grass, which we did not reach till an hour after dark. the wagon was near upsetting several times. how she stood the jolting I cannot imagine. I now hastily pitched my tent, which I gave up for her accomadation, and before morning she was delivered of a little girl.*

James F. Wilkins, 1849

Emigrant names—Carson Pass, California

*. . . I had purposely hastened, that morning, to start ahead of the rest; and not far from noon, I was rewarded by coming out, in advance of all the others, on a rocky height whence I looked, down, far over constantly descending hills, to where a soft haze sent up a warm, rosy glow that seemed to me a smile of welcome; . . . and I knew I was looking across the Sacramento Valley.*

*California, land of sunny skies—that was my first look into your smiling face. I loved you from that moment, for you seemed to welcome me with loving look into rest and safety.*

Sarah Royce, 1849

Oak tree—Hangtown (Placerville), California

Checker-spot butterfly—Yuba Watershed, California

THIS ROUTE WAS OPENED IN 1844 by a company captained by Elisha Stevens. In 1845, the trail was changed to avoid the difficult Truckee River Canyon above Truckee Meadows (Reno). The new route left the river to the northwest from Verdi and went via Dog and Stampede valleys to Truckee's (Donner) Lake. In 1846, a new trail was opened from Truckee's Lake via Coldstream Canyon to the south to avoid the most difficult climb over Donner Pass.

The Stevens-Donner Route, sometimes called the Truckee Route, went from the Humboldt Sink to Sutter's Fort by way of the Truckee River and Donner Pass. As finally evolved, it left the Humboldt Sink almost due west over the Forty Mile Desert. About halfway across this torturous region of alkali flats, hummocks, and sand hills were the Boiling Springs (Brady's Hot Springs), where there was bitter but potable water, though no grass. The next water was to be had only after a merciless stretch beginning with choking dust and ending with deep sands and hard pulling. This part of the desert was often crossed at night to avoid the heat of day. The trail went directly up the narrow canyon of the Truckee River, with many tedious and dangerous fordings. This lower canyon route opened out on Truckee Meadows (Reno), where there were excellent grass and fine views of the Sierra.

The trail continued up the Truckee to Verdi, where it veered north up a steep mountainside to Dog Valley and thence to Stampede Valley, Prosser Creek, and Truckee's Lake. The crest of the Sierra was crossed either via Donner Pass or by Coldstream Canyon, the two routes coming together again at Summit Valley below Lake Mary. From here the trail went almost due west along a granite ridge to Cascade Lakes, where it dropped steeply down the outlet stream into the canyon of the South Yuba River in the vicinity of Cold Springs. It continued down the Yuba a short distance to Big Bend and then left the boulder-strewn river to cross over the mountain to the south of Cisco Butte. It wound across open, manzanita-choked slopes to Carpenter Flat and Emigrant Gap, where wagons had to be let down the precipitous slopes into Bear Valley by ropes. From a point a few miles down Bear Valley the

# The Stevens-Donner Route

Cactus bloom—Forty Mile Desert, Nevada

Desert peak—Forty Mile Desert, Nevada

route sidled up the slope to Deadman's Flat on the top of Lowell Hill Ridge, and from there it wound out the ridge for some distance until it dropped sharply into the Steephollow Crossing. After climbing up from the crossing, the trail dropped ever lower through wooded, hilly terrain, out into the rolling foothills near Bear River Pines and Chicago Park.

The last miles to the first California settlements at the Johnson Ranch (Wheatland) were through the hot, dry, thinly wooded terrain of Cedar Ravine and Wolf Creek. Johnson's Ranch was usually considered to be the actual end of the overland journey, but of course most emigrants continued on the easy forty miles to the American River and Sutter's Fort.

This first of the major wagon routes into California certainly gave the emigrant a full measure of scenery, danger, and hard work. Many were prepared for the difficulty of the eastern ascent, but almost all came to know that for sweat and tears the long descent across the western slopes was equal to anything they had yet experienced.

The route had one great factor in its favor: it was certainly the most direct approach from the Humboldt Sink to the major regions of population in central California. The San Francisco–Sacramento–Reno axis was to be the one along which the future pattern of east-west traffic would be fixed. This geographical factor was enough to ensure continued use of the route, but it certainly did not mean that it was an easy one. Indeed, on a strict mile-for-mile basis, this Stevens-Donner Route must be considered the most difficult of all the major routes. Some were longer and took more time, all had their own special hardships, but none could match this first trail for pure cussedness.

It is one of those quirks of human history that nowhere along this original trans-Sierra route is the name of Elisha Stevens attached to a single topographical feature in order to give him some credit for successfully opening the trail. Chief Truckee is remembered with a town and a beautiful river, but the name of Captain Stevens is nowhere to be found. Instead, the Donner name is attached to every geographical feature of note—the creek, the lake, the peak, the pass. It is perhaps a regrettable but true commentary on the power of the sensational and macabre over the popular mind that the genuine trailblazer is thus completely forgotten and that it is the unfortunate tragedy of the Donner families that is to be forever memorialized on the map of the Sierra. (This is especially so since the Donner group formed only a minority of that entire snowbound contingent of 1846 and didn't even camp with the others at the creek and lake which bear their name.) It is a sad example of human degradation honored and achievement ignored.

Wagon traces—Forty Mile Desert, Nevada

. . . when within 8 or 10 miles of the river I lay down several
times to rest, it did not seam as though I could go any farther
but it was death to stay their so I had to budge along as best I
could thrugh the burning sand till I reached the water. water was
all my wants  I would have given all I possesed for a drink of
cold water  my tongue and lips was parched and fured over so it
took one hour to soak it of.

Charles Tinker, 1849

Boiling Springs (Brady's Hot Springs), Nevada

*May 9, 1846 at about . . . half way from Waushee*
*[Truckee] river to the first water near Mays.*
*Lake still exist a cauldron of Boiling water no*
*stream isues from it [at] present but it stands in*
*several pools Boiling and again disappearing*
*some of these pools have beautiful clear water*
*Boiling in them and others emit Quantities of mud*
*   into one of these muddy pools my little water*
*spaniel Lucky went poor fellow not Knowing*
*that it was Boiling hot he deliberately walked in*
*to the caldron to slake his thirst and cool his*
*limbs when to his sad disappointment and my*
*sorrow he scalded himself allmost insantly to*
*death I felt more for his loss than any other*
*animal I ever lost in my life as he had been my*
*constant companion in all my wandering sine*
*I Left Milwawkee and I vainly hoped to see him*
*return to his old master in his native village*
*(But such is nature of all earthly hopes)*

James Clyman, 1846

Hummocks—Forty Mile Desert, Nevada

Truckee River—Wadsworth, Nevada

*Friday, Sept. 7.... Road very fine—down a valley somewhat sandy, at times crossing immense fields of hard sand, clear & white & looking in the moon light exactly like snow. Took 2 hours rest about midnight & arrived to our great joy at the Salmon Trout River at 7 a.m. on Sunday Sept. 9, & once more had a refreshing draught of pure water ...*

Morning dew—Truckee River, Nevada

Cottonwoods—Truckee River, Nevada

*...& was gladdened by the sight of large majestic trees. The
Salmon Trout being lined with the finest cotton woods I ever saw.
No one can imagine how delightfull the sight of a tree is after
such long stretches of desert, until they have tried it, we have
seen very few of any Kind since leaving the Platte, & what a
luxury after our mules were taken care of, to lay down in their
Shade & make up our two nights loss of sleep, & hear the wind
rustling their leaves & whistling among their branches.*

Elisha Perkins, 1849


*...If ever I saw heaven, I saw it there.*
Lydia Waters, 1855

Sunset— Truckee Meadows (Reno), Nevada

*Monday Sept 10. . . . Our travelling companion Coleman met with quite a loss this p.m. He went down to the ford with his horse & packs & leaving the animal a short time while visiting some of the numerous camps in the vicinity it slipped over a steep bank into the rapid stream below & when Coleman got to the scene of action, the horse had scrambled out but more than half the pack was gone, comprising two valuable broadcloth cloaks, one of which cost 70$, several blankets, an India Rubber spread &c. The fastenings of the pack giving way the articles floated off down the stream, & though we traveled its banks for some miles nothing was rescued but the least valuable cloak, all the poor fellows bedding was lost. He bore it though like a major, & could hardly persuade him to accept of my blanket for the remainder of the trip, seemed to think he could get along well enough with his one cloak. . . .*

*Wednesday Sept 12. . . . Were it not for its serpentine course the Salmon Trout would be a perfect mill race impossible to cross, so rapid is its descent down the mountains. As it is, the force of the current is much broken by friction against the rocks & banks. I have seldom seen so beautiful a stream as this, water clear as crystal, so that standing on an overhanging rock the fish & other objects are easily discernable at the depth of 8 or 10 feet, & being made up of beautiful pools, roaring rapids. For miles in some places it rushes & foams over the rocks & boulders which form its bed, & thus subsides into a still deep pool surrounded by perpendicular walls of rock & evergreen bushes, vine, willows &c. Most lovely spots, & full of fine fish.*

Elisha Perkins, 1849

Truckee River, California

Dog Valley, California

Thistle—Stampede Valley, California

*Friday Sept. 14. . . . We ascended some 4 miles & attained the top from whence we*
*had a fair view of the valley we had left & on yesterday's travel & mountains in the*
*distance, looking immense from our elevated point of observation. . . . Mountain sides*
*here were covered with fine growth of pines, cedars arbor vitae of large size, Firs*
*&c, evergreen bushes of all descriptions formed an undergrowth of great beauty.*
*The contrast to our level sandy dreary roads & parched sage bushes of the last few*
*weeks. Made our mornings previous very exhilirating & delightful & we scrambled*
*on over the mountain road shouting & singing like schoolboys set free.*

Elisha Perkins, 1849

191

Storm building—Verdi, Nevada

*I mooved camp and after a fatiguing day arrivd at ... Starved Camp ... made by the other Compy. who had passed in but a few days previous. here the men began to fail being for several days on half allowance, or 1½ pints of gruel or sizing per day. the sky look like snow and everything indicates a storm god forbid wood being got for the night and Bows for the beds of all, and night closing fast, the clouds still thicking terror terror I feel a terrible foreboding but dare not communicate my mind to any, death to all if our provisions do not come, in a day or two and a storm should fall on us, very cold, a great lamentation about the cold.*

James F. Reed, 1847

Truckee River in winter—California

*Then commenced the ever-to-be-remembered journey up the Truckee to the summit of the Sierras. At first it was not discouraging. There was plenty of wood, water, grass, and game, and the weather was pleasant. The oxen were well rested, and for a few days good progress was made. Then the hills began to grow nearer together, and the country was so rough and broken that they frequently had to travel in the bed of the stream. The river was so crooked that one day they crossed it ten times in traveling a mile. This almost constant traveling in the water softened the hoofs of the oxen, while the rough stones in the bed of the river wore them down, until the cattle's feet were so sore that it became a torture for them to travel. The whole party were greatly fatigued by the incessant labor. But they dared not rest. It was near the middle of October, and a few light snows had already fallen, warning them of the imminent danger of being buried in the snow in the mountains. . . .*

194

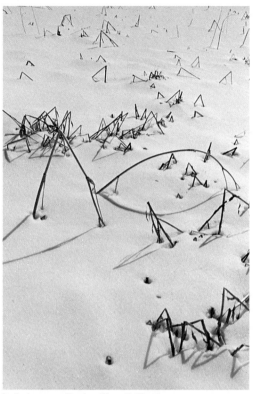

*The snow on the mountains was now about two feet deep. . . . All the wagons were unloaded and the contents carried up the hill. Then the teams were doubled and the empty wagones were hauled up. When about halfway up the mountain they came to a vertical rock about ten feet high. . . . After a tedious search they found a rift in the rock, just about wide enough to allow one ox to pass at a time. Removing the yokes from the cattle, they managed to get them one by one through this chasm to the top of the rock. There the yokes were replaced, chains were fastened to the tongues of the wagons, and carried to the top of the rock, where the cattle were hitched to them. Then the men lifted at the wagons, while the cattle pulled at the chains, and by this ingenious device the vehicles were all, one by one, got across the barrier.*

Moses Schallenberger, 1844

Stalks in snow—Truckee River, California

Donner Pass in early winter—California

Truckee's Lake (Donner Lake), California

*August 25.—About two o'clock, P.M., we suddenly and unexpectedly came in sight of a small lake, some four or five miles in length, and about two miles in breadth. We approached this lake by ascending a small stream which runs through a flat bottom. On every side, except this outlet from it, the lake is surrounded by mountains of great elevation, heavily and darkly timbered with pines, firs, and cedars. The sheet of water just noticed, is the head of Truckee river, and is called by the emigrants who first discovered and named it, Truckee Lake.*

Edwin Bryant, 1846

*Tuesday, August 21st. . . . The old trail went on straight down the valley to the Lake which was distant one mile. I went on to the lake & was fully repaid for my trouble, for it was one of the most beautiful ones on record. It was beautiful, fresh, pure, clear water, with a gravelly bottom, with a sandy beach. It was about 2 miles long, three-quarters wide & confined between three mountains on three sides, which arose immediately from its edge. On the other [side] was the valley by which I had approached it & through which a little stream was passing off from it. I here took a delightful bath & felt renovated.*

Wakeman Bryarly, 1849

Truckee's Lake (Donner Lake), California

197

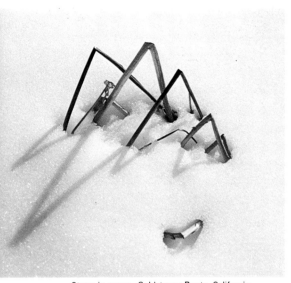

Stems in snow—Coldstream Route, California

*I could go on verry well while i thout we were giting along but as soone as we had to turn back i coud hadley get along but we got to the cabins that night & I froze one of my feet verry bad  that same night thare was the worse storme we had that winter & if we had not come back that night we would never got back  we had nothing to eat but oxhides  o Mary I would cry and wish I had what you all wasted  Eliza had to go to Mr. Graves cabin & we staid at Mr Breen  thay had meat all the time.  & we had to kill littel cash the dog & eat him  we ate his entrails and feet & hide & evry thing about him  o my Dear Cousin you dont now what trubel is yet. Many a time we had on the last thing a cooking and did not now wher the next would come from but there was awl weis some way provided there was 15 in the cabon we was in and half of us had to lay a bed all the time thare was 10 starved to death then  we was hadly abel to walk  we lived on little cash a week and after Mr. Breen would cook his meat we would take the bones and boil them 3 Or 4 days at a time. . . .*

Virginia Reed (age 12), 1847

Spring in snow—Coldstream Route, California

Afternoon clouds—Coldstream Summit, California

Winter snows—Donner Lake, California

Storm clouds—Donner Lake, California

*Thursday 31st  last of the year, may we with Gods help spend the comeing year better than the past which we purpose to do if Almighty God will deliver us from our present dredful situation. . . . morning fair  now Cloudy. . . . looks like another snow storm.*

*Jany. 1st 1847 . . . Commenced snowing last night. . . . sun peeps out at times  provisions geting scant  dug up a hide from under the snow yesterday for Milt.*

*Frid. [January] 26th . . . plenty hides but the folks will not eat them we eat them with a tolerable good apetite. Thanks be to Almighty God.  Amen Mrs Murphy said here yesterday that [she] thought she would commence on Milt. & eat him. I dont [think] that she has done so yet, it is distressing the Donnos told the California folks that they [would] commence to eat the dead people 4 days ago, if they did not succeed that day or next in finding their cattle then under ten or twelve feet of snow & did not know the spot or near it, I suppose they have done so ere this time.*

Patrick Breen, 1846

*Saturday Sept. 15.... The ascent to the pass from Donner cabins is about 5 miles over rocks & steep bluff & through majestic forests of fine cedar. Fir, arbor vitae &c, & a rich luxuriant undergrowth of laurel & various other evergreens. The journey is wild & magnificent beyond description. I was perfectly in raptures during the whole toilsome ascent, & wished often that some of my enthusiastic friends at home, who go into exstacies over our hills could by some air balloons or other labor saving machine be placed by my side. The trees exceeded anything I had ever seen & fully realized my expectations of a Cal. forest. Hundreds of them were six feet in diameter & standing so densely together that I could hardly get myself & mule through them. The road in finding a passage through the trees & among the rocks lengthened the distance to the foot of the pass at least one half.*

*Up, up, we toiled wondering every five minutes how "the dickens" ox teams & wagons can get over here, & it is a wonder indeed, until at 3 p.m. we arrived at the foot of the terrible "Passage on the backbone." For half an hour before arriving we could hear the shouts of teamsters urging their cattle up the steep & when we were near enough to see through the forest we could look up nearly over our heads & see wagons & cattle looking like pigmies, & as if almost suspended in the air. The "Pass" is through a slight depression in the mountains being some 1500 or 2000 feet lower than the tops in its immediate vicinity. As we came up to it the appearance was exactly like marching up to some immense wall built directly across our path so perpendicular is this dividing ridge & the road going up to its very base turns short to the right & ascends by a track cut in the side of the mountains till two thirds up when it turns left again & goes directly over the summit.*

Elisha Perkins, 1849

Coldstream Canyon, California

*Wednesday, August 22nd. . . . We were all in the most joyous & elated spirits this evening. We have crossed the only part of road that we feared, & that without any breakage, loss or detention. I had but the one & only bottle of "cognac" that was in our camp, & which I had managed to keep since leaving the Old Dominion. This I invited my mess to join me in, & which invitation was most cordially accepted. When lo & behold, upon bringing it out, it was empty—yes positively empty. The cork was bad & with numerous joltings, it had gradually disappeared. This was a disappointment many of us will not soon forget.*

Wakeman Bryarly, 1849

Crest of Sierra Nevada from Coldstream Summit, California

Alpine meadow—Coldstream Route, California

*August 19th. . . . North, east and south, peak rose beyond peak in endless succession*
*while in the west the eye looked far down into a chasm where every ravine and*
*gorge shone and glistened with the spotless white of vast snow-fields, and beyond,*
*instead of the expected Sacramento Valley, nothing broke the magnificent expanse*
*of the mountain chains. Thousands of feet down in the chasm—but by no means*
*at the bottom—shone an emerald valley of brightest green, surrounded with snow-fields*
*and intersected by a lovely stream, sparkling from afar on its way through these*
*fastnesses to the golden Sacramento. Probably no human foot had ever before rested*
*on the spot where I stood.*

Isaac Wistar, 1849

White heather—Coldstream Route, California

*Sunday, August 26th. The valley we were in last night properly should be called "Yellow Jacket Valley." Such numbers never were seen before collected together. After building our mess-fire, a nest [was] found directly by us. We were anxious to compromise with them, that if they would let us alone, we would not disturb them. They would not agree, however, & opened hostilities upon us, when we thought it prudent "to raze our eyes" to withdraw our forces under cover. Here we quietly remained until nightfall, when the enemy having retired and reposed in their corall with apparent serenity, we blockaded the mouth of their citadel with a chunk of fire & finished by building our mess fire immediately over their strong & deep founded works. In the morning our mules were scattered in every direction having been run off by these Gulliver little varmints.*

Wakeman Bryarly, 1849

Resting insect—Donner Trail, California

Leaf patterns—Donner Trail, California

Donner Creek, California

Above Donner Lake, California

*Friday, August 24th. . . . We again rolled at 2. Everyone is liable to mistakes, &*
*everyone has a right to call a road* very bad *until he sees a worse. My mistake was*
*that I said I had seen "The Elephant" when getting over the first mountain.*
*I had only seen the tail. This evening I think I saw him in toto. I do not know,*
*however, as I have come to the conclusion that no Elephant upon this route can be so*
*large that another cannot be larger. If I had not seen wagon tracks marked upon*
*the rocks I should not have known there the road was, nor could I have imagined*
*that any wagon & team could possibly pass over in safety.*

Wakeman Bryarly, 1849

Granite cliffs—Donner Pass, California

Summit tree—Donner Pass, California

Morning mists—Alpine Lake, California

*On the top of the mountain we found a beautiful lake [Lake Mary], but quite small, and a few miles farther we came to a fine prairie [Summit Valley]. about three miles long by three-fourths of a mile broad, full of springs and excellent water, and at the lower end a fine branch, which forms the head of Jube river. . . . The difficulty of getting down the mountain was not as great as ascending it, though it was a work of labor, and looked at the first glance as impossible to be performed by horsemen, much more by teams of waggons.*

F. W. Todd, 1845

Bumblebee—Summit Valley, California

*August 21st; on hundred and eleventh day out. Knowing we were over the summit,*
*we started in high spirits this morning, expecting a short, easy down-hill road,*
*but were rudely disappointed, finding ourselves involved in a wild labyrinth of*
*mountains and chasms, with no visible way out. The whole day has been employed*
*in the hardest labor, dragging the wagons over rocky ledges, and hoisting and*
*lowering them over "jump-offs" by "Spanish Windlasses" and other mechanical*
*means. At dark we found ourselves at the top of, and looking down into, a deep,*
*rocky gorge with impassible precipices on either hand. Without knowing what might*
*be at the bottom, we undertook to get the wagons down over the huge boulders which*
*choked the gorge. In lowering the second wagon the rope parted, the wagon flew*
*around and rolled over, bringing up among some small pines many feet below.*
*The entire top was irretrievably demolished, but the important parts seem*
*reparable. The harness is badly broken up, and the wheel mules considerbly cut and*
*bruised. The driver saved himself in a somewhat damaged condition, by jumping*
*over the off-mule and alighting in a bunch of chaparral. We had to camp, strung out*
*along the rocky cleft, just as the catastrophe found us, and by the light of some big*
*fires went to work at the repairs. Occasional guns were discharged as a signal to*
*the water hunters who, notwithstanding the ugly precipices and dense darkness,*
*returned after a long absence in no very joyous humor but with water enough for the*
*men and none for the mules, whose only refreshment tonight is the tough and*
*miscellaneous brush growing among the rocks.*

Isaac Wistar, 1849

Yuba River, California

Bear Valley from Emigrant Gap, California

Pond near Cisco Butte, California

Autumn foliage—Bear Valley, California

*The emigrant wagons of last year were let down this precipice, on the northern side,
with ropes. With considerable difficulty we got our mules down it. A descent of
two miles brought us into a handsome, fertile valley, five or six miles in length, and
varying from one to two in breadth. This is called "Bear valley." Vegetation is very
luxuriant and fresh. In addition to the usual variety of grasses and some flowers, I
noticed large patches of wild peas. We found a small stream winding through it,
bordered by clumps of willows. We encamped near this rivulet of the lonely mountain-
vale, under some tall pines.*

Edwin Bryant, 1846

Wagon ruts—Lowell Hill Ridge, California

Steephollow Crossing, California

Steephollow Crossing, California

*August 28.—A cup of coffee without sugar constituted our breakfast. Our march to-day has been one of great fatigue, and almost wholly without incident or interest. During the forenoon we were constantly engaged in rising and descending the sides of the high mountain ranges, on either hand of the stream, to avoid the canones, deep chasms and ravines, and immense ledges of granite rocks, with which the narrow valley is choked. In the afternoon we travelled along a high ridge, sometimes over elevated peaks, with deep and frightful abysses yawning their darkened and hideous depths beneath us. About five o'clock, P.M., by a descent so steep for a mile and a half, that ourselves and our animals slid rather than walked down it, we entered a small hollow or ravine, which we named "Steep Hollow." A gurgling brook of pure cold water runs through it over a rocky bed. In the hollow there was about a quarter of an acre of pretty good grass, and our mules soon fed this down to its roots, without leaving a blade standing.*

*Having nothing else to do, we made large fires of the dead oak timber that had been cut down by the emigrants of previous years, for the purpose of subsisting their animals upon its foliage. A cup of coffee without sugar, was our supper.*

Edwin Bryant, 1846

Wolf Creek, California

Oak trees, California foothills

*August 26th, Sunday; one hundred and sixteenth day out. Our journey is done, and we hardly know what to do with ourselves, and whether to be glad or sorry. No one took the trouble to stand guard last night, and as we cannot have much more use for the mules, we bore with calmness and fortitude their almost entire deprivation of grass. There will be no more Indian alarms, no more stampedes, no more pulling, carrying and hauling at wagons. Not withstanding ragged clothes and empty stomach, we are all in an exhilarant and joyous mood. The gold is here sure enough, for we have seen it, and we can raise the color ourselves everywhere, even on this very creek. Our census counts ten men, twenty-four mules, three horses and two wagons of our original party and outfit. On the other hand, we are in rags, almost barefooted, without provisions and almost without tools, nearly all of which have been broken to pieces or abandoned. But however sad for the fate of the poor fellows who fell by the way, we are glad to have got here at all.*

Isaac Wistar, 1849

Storm clouds—Central Valley, California

Summit Creek, California

In 1841, THE VERY FIRST of the California emigrant trains, the Bartleson-Bidwell Party, having already abandoned their wagons, crossed the Sierra somewhere in this general vicinity. Their actual route is not known, but the most educated guess places their crossing somewhat to the north of modern Sonora Pass. In 1852, the Clark-Skidmore Party established a passable but most treacherous wagon route from the Walker River across the Sierra to Sonora. This was the Sonora Pass Route of the emigrant, and it crested the Sierra several miles to the south of today's Sonora Pass. In 1853, the Duckwall Party was almost trapped by early snows at Relief Valley but received aid from Sonora in time to struggle through. This near tragedy, plus word of the difficulty of the route, caused it to be largely avoided by emigrant wagons in subsequent years.

The Sonora Route led from the Carson River to Sonora by way of the Walker River, Antelope Valley, Leavitt's Valley, Lower and Upper Relief valleys, and Pinecrest. It left the Mormon-Carson Route in the vicinity of today's Lahontan Reservoir and followed the river southwest to the site of the future Fort Churchill. It then dropped south to the Walker River in Mason Valley and followed it up to where the West Walker came into it through Wilson Canyon. In order to avoid this difficult canyon, the trail swung to the south and then westward over the hills near Mickey Canyon into Smith Valley. From here it proceeded right up the second canyon of the West Walker into Antelope Valley at the base of the main Sierra. Next, it crossed into Little Antelope Valley and climbed over a steep ridge into Lost Cannon Creek, at whose upper end is passed over Summit Meadow and into Leavitt's Meadows.

Apparently, the trail from the upper end of Leavitt's Meadows climbed up the east side of the West Walker for a mile or so and then crossed over to the west side and proceeded directly up to Fremont Lake, which had to be lowered to allow wagons to move along its margins. From there it went up to Emigrant Pass just to the north of Grizzly Peak. Here the trail crossed over open alpine ridges to Emigrant Meadow Lake and thence by Brown Bear Pass and Summit Creek to Relief Creek. (There

# The Sonora Route

Wild rose, Lost Cannon Creek, California

seems to have been a later detour, which dropped down from Emigrant Meadow Lake to Emigrant Lake and then climbed north over the ridge to rejoin the original trail on Summit Creek.)

The trail turned west up Relief Creek to Upper Relief Valley and then down the top of Dodge Ridge to Whiteside Meadow, Burst Rock, and Pinecrest. The final section of the trail wound along the ridge between the South Fork of the Stanislaus and the North Fork of the Tuolumne to Columbia and Sonora.

The Sonora Route was another of those trail-making efforts encouraged by merchant interests in the foothills. In this case, they didn't think it was too feasible until the Clark-Skidmore Party actually proved it could be done in 1852. Encouraged by this success, the town of Sonora sent out an official delegation under the leadership of the mayor the following spring, with instructions to go all the way to the Carson River and try to drum up some traffic for the new road.

The delegates should have known better than to go through with their mission. After all, they had to travel the route eastward and discovered for a certainty just how difficult it was. Nevertheless, they did divert wagons to the new road and the whole affair almost ended with a disaster comparable to the Donner tragedy. A tremendous amount of equipment was destroyed and abandoned in the crossing of this, the most difficult (and most spectacular) of all the trans-Sierra emigrant routes. It deserved the reputation it got from those who struggled across, and it was rejected as a potential wagon route.

Most of the traffic that subsequently did pass over it went in the form of pack trains, and it later enjoyed some considerable popularity as the direct route to the rich Bodie strike in the 1870s. Today, most of the high Sierra portion of this route is still far from the modern highway crossing at Sonora Pass, and even this road has to contend with precipitous grades and rough country. The pass of the emigrants can only be reached on foot or by jeep on old mining roads, and the whole route is a most impressive testimony to the dogged determination of these westering peoples.

Carson River at site of Fort Churchill, Nevada

Walker River canyon above Smith Valley, Nevada

*The place of our camp this evening was a hard, dry country without trees; and there was no wood, except drift which had been brought down by torrents from the mountains, and sage bushes which already began to form a feature in the landscape.*

*The country as we proceeded became more and more sandy and level, and we could see a long distance. There were no bushes, save a little sage and weeds, and no game, save squirrels and praire-dogs.*

Grizzly Adams (Hittell)                    227

Lost Cannon Creek Valley, California

*Having ascended about half a mile, a frightful prospect opened before us:—naked*
*mountains whose summits still retained the snows perhaps of a thousand years:*
*for it had withstood the heat of a long dry summer, and ceased to melt for the season.*
*The winds roared—but in the deep dark Gulfs which yawned on every side,*
*profound solitude seemed to reign.*

John Bidwell, 1841

West branch of West Walker River, California

Leavitt's Valley, California

*We descended suddenly into a large and beautiful valley, and through which wound
the river, now quiet and noiseless.*

*This little valley, or basin, was one of the few truly beautiful spots in this wild
region, containing perhaps thirty or forty acres, and at the northerned extremity a
little miniature lake, the water cool and clear as crystal, and floating upon its surface
was a little flock of ducks, which gave life to the picture. On the south and east,
and rising abruptly from the little grassy meadow, were high barren peaks, while
on the west was a low sandy ridge, over which lay our trail.*

Anonymous, May, 1858
(*Hutching's California Magazine*)

Upper Long Lake, California

Sunrise on the crest of the Sierra Nevada

*The next morning dawned upon a scene beautiful and grand beyond description.*
*Having passed the summit in the night, we returned to the highest point, and arrived*
*there in time to behold the sun rise. Not a cloud obscured the sky, and the ridges of the*
*Sierra, far to the north and far to the south, glittered in their snowy mantles, which,*
*as the sun rose, were flushed with crimson. To the west, faint in the distance, lay*
*the plains of California; to the east, far away stretched hill and dales, lighted up*
*with the russet tints of morning. So enchanting were the views that we remained*
*full an hour enjoying the magnificent prospect.*

Grizzly Adams (Hittell)

Upper Summit Creek Valley, California

*We again pitched our camp for the night, in a grove of cedar near a little bar, which*
*afforded just sufficient grass for our animals for the night. We were now in a truly*
*wild spot, and the mountains on each side of us presented a curious picture, from the*
*fact of their being of such entire opposite formations, and at the same time in*
*such proximity. To our right, and rising abruptly from the branch, the mountain*
*was one unbroken mass of bare granite, its depressions still containing masses of*
*snow, to which Judge and C. climbed and could almost have thrown a snowball into*
*our camp-fire. To the left the ridge was of volcanic formation, and at a distance of*
*three hundred yards from the stream, presented a perpendicular face to the height*
*of twelve hundred feet from the river bed.*

Anonymous, May, 1858
(*Hutching's California Magazine*)

We discovered in several localities in the mountains a kind of wild onion, which was used in flavoring soups made of bones and remnants of meat. After having been so long deprived of vegetables, they were a welcome adjunct to our bill of fare. The Doctor pronounced them healthful, in a general way, and also excellent as a preventative of scurvy, from which we were liable to suffer when living on an exclusive flesh diet, and he advised us to use them freely whenever they could be found. These wild onions were not very large, but what they lacked in size was made up in strength. When eating them in liberal quantities, it is very doubtful whether we would have been cordially received in refined society.

Reuben Shaw, 1849

Wild onions

At 4 o'clock, we descended abruptly into a valley of considerable extent, but, for which we know no name. Here was excellent grass and several little miniature lakes; and, as the margin of one of which attracted our special attention, we concluded to pitch our camp.

It was a thing of rare beauty—a basin scooped out of the solid granite, which here presented a horizontal face of one or two acres, and at the elevation of several feet above the surrounding valley, without inlet or outlet, and with a depth of some three feet, its water cool and clear as crystal. On the east side, was a little plat of grass, and here we picketed our horses, while for ourselves, we selected a cosy little nook just a few rods to the south, where we built a cheerful fire and spread our blankets with a breastwork of rock on either side.

Anonymous, May, 1858
(*Hutching's California Magazine*)

Upper Relief Valley, California

Mount Shasta from the site of Fort Reading, California

THIS ROUTE WAS DISCOVERED IN 1851 by William Nobles while searching for gold. In 1852, the first emigrants were diverted to this route at Great Meadows (Lassen's Meadows) on the Humboldt River. It proved to be a very easy route for wagons. In 1856, this route was shortened by the discovery of a hot springs midway between Rabbithole Springs and Granite Springs at its eastern end.

Nobles' Route ran from the Applegate-Lassen Trail at the Great Boiling Springs at Black Rock Point to Shasta City, by way of the Smoke Creek Desert and Lassen Peak.

The original Nobles' Trail followed the Applegate-Lassen Route to the Great Boiling Springs at Black Rock Point. It then cut westward across a finger of Black Rock Desert and dropped south along the eastern base of the Granite Range to water and grass at Granite Springs. From there it proceeded past the Hot Springs at Gerlach (discovered by Frémont in 1844) and rounded the point of the Granite Range to move along the watering places on the western edge of Smoke Creek Desert.

The emigrant next wound up Smoke Creek Canyon to the lower end of Smoke Creek Meadows and thence westward over the low divide into the valley of Rush Creek. The next stop was to the south and west at Mud Springs and then on to Honey Lake Valley and the Susan River at Susanville. The trail left Susanville (first known as Roop's Fort) to the northwest and climbed through dense pines and cedars to Feather Lake, where it met the Lassen Trail.

At this junction the emigrant had a choice of either going on to Shasta City or cutting over by the older trail to Lassen's Rancho, which was considerably farther south in the Great Valley. Nobles' Route itself coincided with Lassen's Trail as far as Grays Valley or Poison Lake, and then it turned westward to Butte Creek and up the creek to Butte Lake and Black Butte (Cinder Cone). Volcanic sands made the next few miles west to Badger Flat hard going, but then the trail turned up Hat Creek through forests and meadows.

At the base of Lassen Peak, the route turned north down Lost Creek and then west over the first-named Nobles' Pass to Manzanita Lake.

# The Nobles Route

Black Rock Springs, Nevada

(Very soon, a detour—to avoid difficult roads and lingering snows—was opened from a point just beyond Badger Flat, and it struck off down Hat Creek to Emigrant Ford before swinging over to Lost Creek and around Table Mountain to ascend the second Nobles' Pass and rejoin the original route at the Manzanita Chute below Manzanita Lake.) From that point, the trail dropped down through Deer Flat, Mountain Home, McCumber's on Millseat Creek, Grace Lake, Shingletown, Shingle Creek, Lack Creek, Bear Creek, Cow Creek, the Sacramento River near Fort Reading, and Shasta City.

An important improvement on Nobles' Route was the opening of a cutoff directly from Rabbithole Springs to Granite Springs by way of a hot springs which was discovered at the base of the Semenite Range about midway between those two points. The difficult loop up to Black Rock Point was thus rendered unnecessary. The discovery of this important cutoff is credited to two prospectors in the year 1856, but curiously enough, as early as 1849 Bruff records a report to the effect that these hot springs existed and that a trail just might be possible in that direction. Fortunately for them, none of the emigrants of that season chose to follow up on the rumor, although some of them might have been sorely tempted if they could just have foreseen what lay ahead of them on the Lassen Trail. In 1849, no one had effectively explored that vast area between Rabbithole and the Sacramento Valley, and anyone striking out blindly with only a rumor to go on was courting tragedy. At first glance, such restraint and prudence on the part of the emigrants, and especially the gold seekers of that first year of the Gold Rush, might seem very remarkable, but the real explanation for their lack of interest probably lay in their misapprehension that they were already truly on a great shortcut that promised to land them all nicely in California in only a few more days.

There can be no question that this route of Nobles' was to prove the easiest of all the routes into California after it was opened. It was also very much in the spirit of the times, being one of those "commercial routes," opened expressly for the purpose of funneling emigrants into a particular region of the Great Valley. In this case the destination was the town of Shasta at the very head of the Sacramento Valley. Not only did this route become almost immediately successful but, unlike poor Beckwourth, Nobles was able to collect some $2,000 for his trailblazing efforts.

All during the 1850s and '60s it remained a favorite route for both emigrants and cattle drives, and even for a time threatened to be competitive with the central Sierra crossings. But in the end—despite the fact that one of the main rail lines was to be built within sight of long stretches of it—it proved to be just too remote from the main population centers. Today, it is little more than a series of dirt and gravel roads over much of its length, a pathetic little echo of what it would most certainly have been if chance had only located it a hundred miles to the south.

Black Rock Desert, Nevada

*August 17. As I walked on slowly and with effort, I encountered a great many
animals, perishing for want of food and water, on the desert plain. Some would be
gasping for breath, others unable to stand, would issue low moans as I came up,
in a most distressing manner, showing intense agony; and still others, unable to walk,
seemed to brace themselves up on their legs to prevent falling, while here and there
a poor ox, or horse, just able to drag himself along, would stagger towards me with
a low sound as if begging for a drop of water. My sympathies were excited at
their sufferings, yet, instead of affording them aid, I was a subject for relief myself.*

*High above the plain, in the direction of our road, a black, bare mountain reared its
head, at the distance of fifteen miles; and ten miles this side the plain was flat,
composed of baked earth, without a sign of vegetation, and in many places covered
with incrustations of salt. Pits had been sunk in moist places, but the water was
salt as brine, and utterly useless. . . .*

Alonzo Delano, 1849

Antelope, vicinity of Susanville, California

We saw to-day several large white wolves, and two herds of antelopes. The latter is
one of the most beautiful animals I ever saw. When full grown, it is nearly as large
as a deer. The horns are rather short, with a single prong near the top, and an
abrupt backward curve at the summit like a hook. The ears are very delicate, almost
as thin as paper, and hooked at the tip like the horns. The legs are remarkably
slender and beautifully formed, and as it bounds over the plain, it seems scarcely to
touch the ground, so exceedingly light and agile are it's motions.

J. K. Townshend, 1834

After leaving the creek we passed two or three small ponds, and
entered one of the most recently formed and strongly marked
volcanic fields we have seen in these mountains. It occupies a
valley of three or four miles in length, by one or one and a half in
width. The lava rocks are black, and about 100 feet high, occupying
the valley in a confused mass, which it would be difficult to cross
on foot. On the north side of this field stands the Black Butte,
some 800 or 1,000 feet high. It is conical from its base upwards
for several hundred feet, and is terminated in a peak with a
semi-sperical outline; and its whole surface as black as the darkest
iron ore, is covered with a coarse, pebbly sand, formed from its
crumbling mass, which has so smoothed its surface that a pebble
would roll from its summit uninterruptedly to its base.

Lieutenant Beckwith, 1854

Black Butte (Cinder Cone), Butte Lake, California

Aspen trunk, Lost Creek, California

*Immediately after leaving the valley, you enter open, but heavy pine woods —not unwelcome to the sun-scorched emigrant—and commence ascending the Sierra Nevada gradually; water four miles on the right, and some grass; and again five miles on the left, but no grass; the road somewhat stony in places; the ascent is so gradual that on slight observation it seem as much down as up; in fact, a great part is level, and enough timber on one mile on each side of the road, from the valley to the summit, to build a double railway track to the Missouri River.*

John Dreibelbis, 1853

Gentian, Feather Lake, California

Badger Meadows, Lassen National Park, California

Volcanic terrain, Upper Sacramento Valley, California

Sacramento River crossing, Anderson, California

*About daybreak the following morning*
*the hoarse howling of a wolf, and*
*the loud snapping and whining bark*
*of some coyotes awoke us. Before us*
*lay the broad Lassen's Meadows,*
*entirely surrounded by low timbered*
*ridges; and in the distance, bold,*
*grand, and cold, towered Lassen's*
*Butte; but when the sun arose and*
*gilded it with rosy, gold sunlight, it*
*was gorgeous—it was magnificent.*

John Dreibelbis, 1853
(*Hutching's California Magazine*)

Manzanita Chute, near Second Nobles' Pass, California

Long Creek, California

THIS ROUTE WAS DISCOVERED and opened by the famous mulatto mountain man, James Beckwourth, in 1851. It was first traveled by emigrants in 1852.

Beckwourth's route led from the Truckee River at Truckee Meadows (Reno) to Marysville in the Sacramento Valley by way of Beckwourth Pass and the Feather River. It left the Stevens-Donner Trail at Truckee Meadows, just at the eastern base of the Sierra, and ran north along the route generally followed today by U.S. 395. The trail dipped through Lemmon and Cold Spring valleys and led northward along Long Valley Creek to Beckwourth Pass and an easy climb over sage slopes into Sierra Valley and the headwaters of the Middle Fork of the Feather River. After proceeding along the north edge of Sierra Valley, the trail turned up Grizzly Creek to Grizzly Valley and thence westward through Three Mile Valley, Happy Valley, Long Valley, and Spring Garden Valley to American Valley and Quincy. From here, the route was over to Elizabethtown, up Emigrant Hill to Snake Lake Valley, Spanish Creek, Meadow Valley,

and Buck's Lake. It then began the long drop down the ridge between the North and Middle forks of the Feather River, passing through Junction House, Mountain House, Berry Creek, and Bidwell's Bar. From Bidwell's Bar, the trail branched west to Oroville and south to Marysville, at the confluence of the Feather and Yuba rivers.

Very soon after this original route was established, another shorter but more rugged route was opened to Marysville by way of the ridge lying between the South Fork of the Feather and the North Fork of the Yuba. This trail left the upper Feather River at Blairsden and proceeded to Johnsville, Jamison Creek, Gibsonville, La Porte, Strawberry Valley, Forbestown, and Marysville. This was a difficult route and probably saw more pack trains and gold seekers than emigrant wagons.

The Beckwourth Pass Route was unquestionably one of the easiest crossings into California. Indeed, the pass itself hardly qualified as more than a hill in the parlance of the trail-experienced emigrant, and the long drop down the western slopes presented no special prob-

# The Beckwourth Route

Leopard lily, American Valley, California

lems. One can readily see why, as both a wagon and cattle route, it seems to have won immediate favor and carried a great deal of traffic in the 1850s and '60s. It was only with the firm establishment of the preeminence of the Sacramento–Donner Pass/Tahoe Basin Corridor that it suffered a sharp decline, as did all the other trails.

James Beckwourth was one of the most colorful of that breed of frontiersmen known as mountain men—a group that didn't lack for color at any level. The son of a planter and a Negro slave, he had trapped and traveled the West in search of fortune and adventure, and had gone native and lived among the Crow Indians for many years.

Beckwourth had come to California because of the chance for wealth, and he was quick to see the financial possibilities of an easy trail across the Sierra. While all the previous trans-Sierra routes had been influenced to some extent by the location of the settlements in California, his was the first to be opened especially to feed emigrants and their business into the new towns that had sprung up in the gold regions of the Sierra foothills. He had plotted his route and then verbally contracted with the merchants of Marysville, Oroville, and the American Valley (Quincy) to open a trail that would benefit them. He received a few hundred dollars as down payment from the merchants of Marysville and set out for the Truckee to gather up some emigrants.

He brought them through in good style, but unfortunately for him, Marysville immediately burned to the ground, and the merchants were not able to pay the balance they owed him. In fact, according to Beckwourth's reckoning, he had spent a considerable amount of money from his own pocket to get the trail improved for wagon travel. He took his empty pockets and settled for a short time in Sierra Valley, just west of the pass that was to bear his name. There he would be the first to greet the emigrant along his route and do a little profitable trading as well.

Long Creek Valley, California

Beckwourth's Pass, California

*While on this excursion I discovered what is now known as "Beckwourth's Pass"*
*in the Sierra Nevada. From some of the elevations over which we passed I remarked*
*a place far away to the southward that seemed lower than any other. I made no*
*mention of it to my companion, but thought that at some future time I would*
*examine into it farther. . . .*

*On my return to the American Valley [Quincy], I made known my discovery to a*
*Mr. Turner, proprietor of the American Ranch, who entered enthusiastically into*
*my views; it was a thing, he said, he had never dreamed of before. If I could but*
*carry out my plan, and divert travel into that road, he thought I should be a made*
*man for life. Thereupon he drew up a subscription-list, setting forth the merits of the*
*project, and showing how the road could be made practicable to Bidwell's Bar, and*
*thence to Marysville, which latter place would derive peculiar advantages from the*
*discovery. He headed the subscription with two hundred dollars.*

*When I reached Bidwell's Bar and unfolded my project, the town was seized with*
*a perfect mania for the opening of the route. The subscriptions toward the fund*
*required for its accomplishment amounted to five hundred dollars.*

James Beckwourth

Prickly poppy, Beckwourth's Pass, California

Tarweed, Sierra Valley, California

Marsh marigold, Jamison Creek, California

Sierra Valley, California

*It was the latter end of April when we entered upon an extensive valley at the north-west extremity of the Sierra range. The valley was already robed in freshest verdure, contrasting most delightfully with the huge snow-clad masses of rock we had just left. Flowers of every variety and hue spread their variegated charms before us; magpies were chattering, and gorgeously-plumaged birds were caroling in the delights of unmolested solitude.*

James Beckwourth

Antelope, Sierra Valley, California

*Swarms of wild geese and ducks were swimming on the surface of the cool crystal stream, which was the central fork of the Rio de las Plumas, or sailed the air in clouds over our heads. Deer and antelope filled the plains, and their boldness was conclusive that the hunter's rifle was to them unknown. Nowhere visible were any traces of the white man's approach, and it is probably that our steps were the first that ever marked the spot. We struck across this beautiful valley to the waters of the Yuba, from thence to the waters of the Truchy, which latter flowed in an easterly direction, telling us we were on the eastern slope of the mountain range.*

James Beckwourth

Ducks, Sierra Valley, California

In the spring of 1852 I established myself in Beckwourth Valley, and finally found myself transformed into a hotel-keeper and chief of a trading-post. My house is considered the emigrant's landing-place, as it is the first ranch he arrives at in the golden state, and is the only house between this point and Salt Lake. . . . When the weary, toil-worn emigrant reaches this valley, he feels himself secure; he can lay himself down and taste refreshing repose, undisturbed by the fear of Indians. His cattle can graze around him in pasture up to their eyes, without running any danger of being driven off by the Arabs of the forest, and springs flow before them as pure as any that refreshes this verdant earth. . . .

At the close of day, perhaps amid a pelting rain, these same parties heave wearily into sight: they have achieved the passage of the Plains, and their pleasant Eastern homes, with their agreeable, sociable neighbors, are now at a distance it is painful to contemplate. The brave show they made at starting, as the whole town hurraed them off, is sadly faded away. Their wagon appears like a relic of the Revolution after doing hard service for the commissariat: its cover burned into holes, and torn to tatters; its strong axles replaced with rough pieces of trees hewn by the wayside; the tires bound on with ropes; the iron linch-pins gone, and chips of hickory substituted, and rags wound round the hubs to hold them together, which they keep continually wetted to prevent falling to pieces. The oxen are held up by the tail to keep them upon their legs, and the raven and magpies evidently feel themselves ill treated in being driven off from what they deem their lawful rights.

The old folks are peevish and quarrelsome; the young men are so headstrong, and the small children so full of wants, and precisely at a time when every thing has given out, and they have nothing to pacify them with. But the poor girls have suffered the most. Their glossy, luxuriant locks, that won so much admiration, are now frizzled and discolored by the sun; their elegant riding-habit is replaced with an improvised Bloomer, and their neat little feet are exposed in sad disarray; their fingers are white no longer, and in place of rings we see sundry bits of rag wound round, to keep the dirt from entering their sore cuts. The young men of gold, who looked so attractive in the distance, are now too often found to be worthless and of no intrinsic value; their time employed in haunting gaming-tables or dram-shops, and their habits corrupted by unthrift and dissipation.

James Beckwourth

*I was destined to disappointment, for that same night Marysville was laid in ashes. The mayor of the ruined town congratulated me upon bringing a train through. He expressed great delight at my good fortune, but regretted that their recent calamity had placed it entirely beyond his power to obtain for me any substantial reward. With the exception of some two hundred dollars subscribed by some liberal-minded citizens of Marysville, I have received no indemnification for the money and labor I have expended upon my discovery. The city had been greatly benefited by it, as all must acknowledge, for the emigrants that now flock to Marysville would otherwise have gone to Sacramento. Sixteen hundred dollars I expended upon the road is forever gone, but those who derive advantage from this outlay and loss of time devote no thought to the discoverer; nor do I see clearly how I am to help myself, for every one knows I can not roll a mountain into the pass and shut it up. But there is one thing certain: although I recognize no superior in love of country, and feel in all its force the obligation imposed upon me to advance her interest, still, when I go out hunting in the mountains a road for every body to pass through, and expending my time and capital upon an object from which I shall derive no benefit, it will be because I have nothing better to do.*

James Beckwourth

Sierra Nevada at Jamison Creek, California

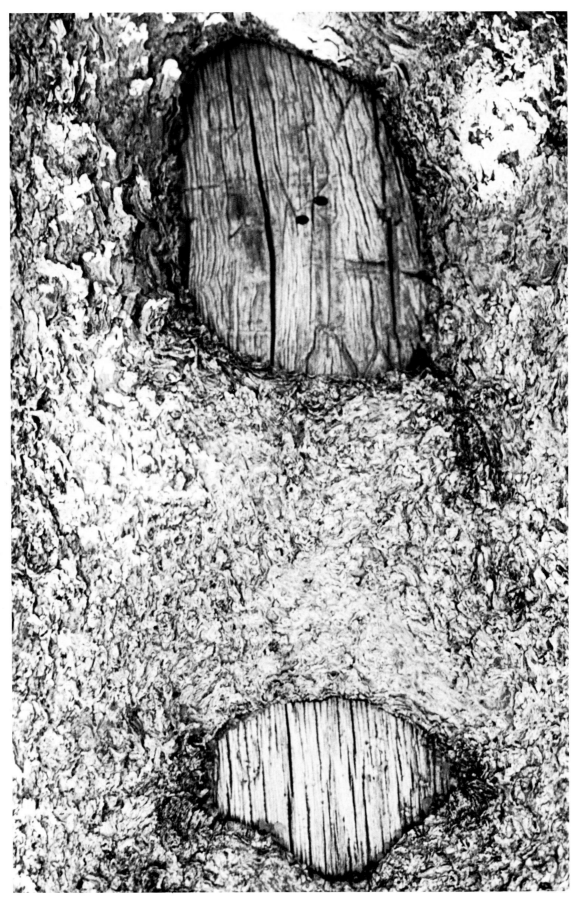

Emigrant blazes, Upper Relief Valley, California

# APPENDIX

# BIOGRAPHICAL SKETCHES
## OF THE EMIGRANTS QUOTED IN "A PICTORIAL JOURNEY"

**Adams, "Grizzly."** Born Massachusetts in 1812. His parents named him John, but he took the name of his brother, James Capen Adams. Trains as shoemaker but prefers the wilderness. Comes to California in 1849 and takes turns at mining, ranching, shopkeeping, and shoemaking. Finally, he goes to the mountains and becomes legendary for his exploits in fighting, capturing, and training wild animals. Opens animal museum in San Francisco in 1855 and in 1860 takes it to New York, where he becomes a partner of P. T. Barnum. Dies very shortly after reaching New York of complications from an old skull wound received fighting a grizzly.

**Applegate, Lindsay.** Born Kentucky in 1808. Brother of Jesse Applegate, another Oregon pioneer. Went to Oregon in the migration of 1843. In 1846 helps to open the Applegate Trail into southern Oregon. Resided in several localities in Oregon as business needs demanded. Active in state affairs: farmer, businessman, state legislator, militia leader, Indian agent. Dies in Oregon in 1892. The Applegate family was very prominent in Oregon society.

**Beckwourth, James P.** Born in Virginia in 1798; mother was a black woman, father a planter. He becomes a mountain man and lives with the Crow Indians for many years. First goes to California in 1844 as a trader. Returns to California in 1848 and dictates autobiography which is published in 1856. He is back in Missouri in 1859 and then goes to Denver, where he is a storekeeper, farmer, saloonkeeper. Also employed as scout and advisor to the army in dealings with local Indians. Takes part in the Sand Creek Massacre. Gives up farming and goes back to trapping and scouting. Legend has it that he died back among the Crows in 1866.

**Bidwell, John.** Born in New York in 1819. As a young teacher, he was one of the moving forces behind the organization of the first wagon train to California in 1841. Upon reaching California, he works for Captain Sutter for several years at Fort Ross, Hock Farm, and Sutter's Fort. He strikes gold at Bidwell's Bar on Feather River. This is the foundation of his great fortune. He buys Chico Ranch in 1849 and eventually expands it to twenty-six thousand acres. Elected member of first state senate in 1849 and to U.S. Congress in 1864. Runs unsuccessfully three times for governor and is the 1892 Prohibition Party candidate for president of the United States. Donates land for Chico Normal School, which is to become Chico State College. Dies in 1900.

**Breen, Patrick.** Born in Ireland and comes to Canada in 1828. Moves to U.S. in 1833—first to Illinois and then Iowa. Comes to California in 1846 and is trapped for the winter in the Sierra with the ill-fated Donner Party. His entire family survives the ordeal. After recuperating at Sutter's Fort, he starts looking for a home and settles in San Juan Valley at Mission San Juan Bautista. His home becomes a well-known inn for travelers. He and his family become prominent landowners in valley. Becomes supervisor of Monterey County. He dies in 1868.

**Bruff, J. Goldsborough.** Born in Washington, D.C., in 1804. Attends West Point but doesn't graduate. Joins the navy and goes to sea for a few years, and then becomes a draftsman for the federal government and remains in that capacity—except for a brief hiatus in California—for some sixty years. He is the captain of a train of gold-seekers in 1849 by the Lassen Route. He returns via Panama in 1851 after considerable travels to the various gold regions of state but with little luck. He hopes to have his journals published, but they aren't published until 1944. He dies in 1889, leaving behind one of the great records of the 1849 crossings.

**Bryant, Edwin.** Born in Massachusetts in 1805. Moves to Kentucky and, although he had studied medicine as a young man, he becomes a journalist. He journeys to California in 1846, both to improve health and gather material for a book. His book, published in 1849 and called *What I Saw in California*, was well-written and widely read in that gold fever year. Upon reaching California, he helps organize a group of emigrants to take part in the rebellion and serves as one of its officers.

After campaign, he is appointed alcalde of San Francisco. (Bryant Street in San Francisco is named for him.) Returns to Kentucky in 1847. In 1849, he leads a party of gold-seekers to California again. In 1853, he returns to Kentucky for good. He is by then very comfortably fixed financially, but in 1869, he ends his own life.

**Bryarly, Wakeman.** Born in Maryland in 1820. Trained as a physician. Goes to California in 1849, is in emigrating company captained by B. F. Washington. Practices as physician and, because of his Democratic loyalties, receives several patronage appointments in state. Returns to Maryland in 1855 and marries. Volunteers for service with the Russians in the Crimean War and serves there for a few months. Returns to California and then to Virginia City in Nevada, where he practices medicine. Returns to Maryland and dies in 1869.

**Clyman, James.** Born in Virginia in 1792. Moves to Ohio and then Pennsylvania, and learns to be a surveyor. In 1823 goes to work for William Ashley of fur trade repute. He becomes a trapper and mountain man, and fights in the Black Hawk War of 1832–33. He then pioneers in Wisconsin. In 1844, he decides to join emigration to Oregon. Travels on to California and returns to States in 1846. He leads emigrant train to California in 1848. He marries and settles down on a fruit and dairy ranch in the Napa Valley. Dies in 1881. His diaries are considered classics.

**Delano, Alonzo.** Born in New York State in 1806. Marries in 1831. Moves to Indiana and opens a general store; then to Illinois. Journeys to California in 1849. He has little luck mining, so goes into land speculation, trading with Indians, and writing for newspapers. Moves to Grass Valley in 1851 to mine. Does well enough to go east to visit family. Returns with them to Grass Valley. The town burns down, and there is a panic in 1855, but he goes into banking and mining, and prospers. He becomes a very popular writer, notably for his humorous stories on mining life. His book on crossing published in 1854. Also publishes *Old Block's Sketch Book*, which was very successful. He becomes leading community figure and reweds after wife's death. Dies in 1874.

**Dreibelbis, John.** No record except that he is quoted as the source of guide for Nobles' Trail in *Hutching's California Magazine*.

**Frémont, John Charles.** Born in Virginia in 1813. He receives a commission in the U.S. Corps of Topographical Engineers in 1838. He marries Jessie Benton, daughter of Sen. Thomas Hart Benton, in 1841 and thus establishes powerful political connections. Leads Topographical Expeditions for U.S. Army in 1842, 1843, and 1845 to the West. He happens to be in California in 1845 when the Bear Flag Revolt breaks out, and he takes a very active part in securing the region for the United States. He is returned east and court-martialed for disobedience and mutiny for refusing to obey his superiors. He is found guilty but is not punished and is allowed to resign. He leads a disastrous private expedition to the Rockies in 1848. He returns to California in 1848 to his gold rich Mariposa Grant (bought in 1847). Elected U.S. Senator from California in 1849. In 1856, he is the first Republican candidate for president, but loses to Buchanan. Bad investments cause him to lose Mariposa property. In Civil War, he is appointed commander of the West and then relieved of command for improprieties. He is offered a lesser command but chooses to resign. Continues to have financial reverses and is mostly supported by wife's earnings as a writer. He dies in 1890 in New York.

**Frizzell, Lodisa.** Little record except that she journeys to California in 1852 with her husband and four sons. She wrote her journal in December of that year.

**Geiger, Vincent.** Born in Maryland in 1823 or 1824. He is a small businessman in his hometown. He joins company—along with Bryarly—which was led by B. F. Washington, and they cross in 1849. In California, he first

becomes a trader and a lawyer, and then joins with Washington as coeditor of the *Sacramento Democratic State Journal*. He becomes heavily involved in Democratic politics in the state and is appointed Indian agent and also is elected Democratic state chairman. He leaves newspaper business. He kills a man in a drunken brawl in Red Bluff and flees state. He dies in Valparaiso, Chile, in 1869.

**Gould, Jane Holbrook.** Born in Ohio in 1833. She is married in 1852, and leaves from Iowa for California with her husband and two sons in 1862. They enter California by the Big Trees Route. Her husband dies five months after arrival.

**Green, Jay.** No record.

**Hastings, Lansford W.** Leaves Ohio as a twenty-three-year-old lawyer in 1842 when he journeys to Oregon in the party led by Dr. Elijah White. He is chosen to replace White as captain at Fort Laramie. Leaves Oregon and travels to California in 1843. In 1844 returns to States via Mexico and in 1845 publishes his *Guide*. Returns overland to California in late 1845 and helps lay out town of Sutterville (Sacramento) for Captain Sutter. Returns east in spring of 1846, opening up his Cutoff across the Salt Lake Desert. (This is the route of the ill-fated Reed-Donner Party.) Hastings himself leads the Harlan-Young Party to California by this route and by late 1846 is a captain in Frémont's California Battalion. After revolution, he practices law and marries, in addition to taking an active part in the political arena. In 1863 he joins Confederate cause with a proposal to take Arizona from the Union. After Civil War he promotes a scheme to settle former Confederates in Brazil, where he dies in 1870.

**Hopkins, Sarah Winnemucca.** Born about 1844 in the Humboldt Sink area. She was the granddaughter of Captain Truckee, the friend and early guide to emigrants. She has several years education at a convent in San Jose, California. Over the years, she has several jobs with the U.S. Government, mostly dealing with her people, the Paiutes. In 1878, she acts as an agent for the U.S. Army in the Bannock Uprising, and is praised for her service. When the Paiutes are ordered off their lands to the Yakima Reservation in Washington Territory, Sarah begins lecturing against the bad treatment of her people, first in San Francisco and then in the East. Several prominent women take up her cause, and she wins promises in Washington of succor. It never comes. She becomes the center of a controversy when an Indian agent accuses her of being a common prostitute. She travels to Montana and marries a shadowy figure named Hopkins. In 1883, she goes east to lecture and to make an appeal to Congress. Returns to open Indian school in Lovelock in 1889. Begins to fail in health and takes up gambling. Dies on a visit to her sister in Montana in 1891.

**Ingalls, Eleaser Stillman.** No record.

**Jefferson, T. H.** Almost nothing known of the man. He traveled to California in 1846 via the Hastings Route (the same route the Donner Party was to use) and compiled a map of the route. The map appeared in 1849—along with a practical accompaniment—as a guide. He based his map on the earlier one of Frémont, but his was drawn for day-to-day use and covered regions which Frémont had not covered. It is considered one of the best of all the trail maps.

**Johnston, Wm. G.** Journeys to California from Pennsylvania in 1849. He returns home in the same year via Panama. Apparently, Johnston was one of those who made the journey mostly as a lark. He worked only halfheartedly at mining and talked of going on to new adventures in China and the Sandwich Islands (Hawaii). He chose not to winter at the mines and headed for home, where he frankly admits that he enjoyed being lionized for several weeks. He returned to California by train in 1891 to revisit the scene of his great adventure.

**Kelly, William.** Little is known of this English writer except that he left England in 1849 and joined Colonel Russell's party of that same year for the journey to California. They traveled by the Humboldt and Carson River routes to Weber Creek, and then he traveled extensively throughout the various gold regions in order to write about he saw. The book is a mine of literate observations about life in California in those days.

**Langworthy, Franklin.** Born in Vermont in 1798. Moves to New York State, becomes Universalist minister, and marries. Moves to Illinois. Journeys to California in 1850. Has little luck or inclination to mine. Travels about supporting himself by lecturing on various scientific and philosophical subjects. He avows that he really just wanted to see the wonders of the West. He returns to East via Central America in 1853. His book is published in New York in 1855. He dies in Minnesota before 1859.

**Leonard, Zenas.** Born in Pennsylvania in 1809. Always attracted to the wilderness from early youth. He becomes a mountain man and free trapper, and writes an account of his western adventures, including the trip down the Humboldt and over the Sierra with the Walker Party in 1833–34. He returns to Pennsylvania in 1835, and then moves on to Missouri, where he marries, has children, and runs various businesses. He dies in 1857.

**Moorman, Madison Berryman.** Born in Kentucky in 1824. He journeys to California in 1850, when he is twenty-six and still single. He has little luck in the gold fields and soon returns to live in Tennessee. He becomes a successful cotton broker. He is antislavery and pro-Unionist in his personal sentiments, but refuses to fight for either side in the Civil War. He dies in 1915.

**Parkman, Francis.** Born 1823 in Massachusetts to an old family. He was in ill-health most of his life but forced himself to endure outdoor life. He graduates from Harvard Law School and determines to write a great history of the United States. To get background material on Indian lore and ways, he travels with his equally young cousin to Fort Laramie and the Indian Territories in 1846. He goes on to an illustrious career as a historian. He is still considered one of the greatest American historians, and one of the first to attempt fieldwork. He dies in 1893.

**Perkins, Elisha Douglass.** Born in Connecticut in 1823. His family moves to Ohio in 1839, and—as a young man, newly married and with considerable education—he finds it hard to find a suitable job. He journeys to California in 1849 to find enough of a fortune to get a start for himself and his newly pregnant wife. He finds little gold, and his health begins to deteriorate. He gives up mining and becomes a steamboat captain on the Sacramento River. He dies of dysentery in 1852 and is buried in Sacramento.

**Platt, P. L. and N. Slater.** Platt crosses in the years 1849 and '50. Slater crosses in 1850 and '51. Their *Guide* is published in 1852. Platt becomes a doctor and lawyer in the Mother Lode. Slater, who is a teacher and minister, reaches Placerville in 1851 and becomes very prominent in education. He serves as the county superintendent of schools of Sacramento County.

**Preuss, Charles.** Born in Germany in 1803. Serves as chief cartographer to Frémont on his first and second western expeditions and also takes part in the disastrous fourth one. He journeys to California in 1849 and works for some time as a surveyor. He suffers a sunstroke in 1850 and returns to Washington to live. He again takes up cartography and becomes a draftsman on the Pacific Railroad survey in 1853. Unable to fulfill his duties, he returns to his home in Washington and commits suicide in 1854.

**Pritchard, James A.** Born in Kentucky in 1816. Journeys to California in 1849 and has some success in the gold fields. He loses everything in a flash flood while returning to Kentucky in 1851 with the exception of one small bag of gold. He moves to Missouri in 1852 and becomes a country squire. He enters state politics as a Whig and is elected. When the Civil War comes, he becomes a colonel in the Confederate army and dies in 1862 of wounds received in battle.

**Read, George Willis.** Read was a physician in Pennsylvania before captaining a train to California in 1850. He hasn't much luck in diggings and becomes quite sick. He turns to fruit and grain ranching, and invests in mining ventures. He prospers and returns to the East to visit family in 1856 and 1862. On returning to California via Panama in 1862, his ship is captured by a Confederate gunboat. He is back in California in 1863 and crosses the U.S. on the transcontinental railroad in 1869. He dies in California in 1880.

**Reed, James F.** Born in Ireland. Journeys to California in 1846 with the Donner contingent. His family is trapped at Donner Lake, but because he had been previously banished from traveling with the train for killing John Snyder in a quarrel, he had already crossed the Sierra before them. When he finds he can't get back to them because of the snows, he serves a stint in the California Rebellion and goes about collecting funds and organizing efforts for the relief expeditions. He gets through to his family with the second relief party and finds them all alive. He had carried money with him to California, and he does well in the gold fields. He invests it in land around San Jose, where the family goes to live. He becomes wealthy and is elected to public offices. He dies in 1874.

**Reed, Virginia.** Virginia becomes a Catholic as she had vowed she would do if she survived their ordeal. She marries John M. Murphy, who came to California in the Stevens Party of 1844, and they remain in California. She dies in 1921.

**Remy, Jules.** French natural scientist and writer who travels to Salt Lake City in 1855 especially to write a book on Mormonism. He starts from California and returns there on his way back to France. The English version of his book is published in 1861. Mormonism is of great interest to everyone in this period, and Remy considers himself an on-the-spot investigative reporter. It is interesting that this French writer had his book published in England, where a great deal of very successful Mormon proselytizing was in progress at the time.

**Royce, Sarah.** Born in England. She comes to New York and journeys to California in 1849. They spend a short time in the mines and then move to San Francisco and the Bay Area for three years. They move back to the Mother Lode and settle at Grass Valley. After twelve years in that mining community, they return to live in San Francisco. The Royces' son, Josiah, who was born in California, went on to become one of the great American philosophers, writers, and teachers.

**Schallenberger, Moses.** As a teen-age member of the Stevens Party of 1844, Moses spends the winter alone at Donner Lake and survives. It is one of the truly remarkable episodes of the entire emigrant era. He becomes a clerk and trader at Sutter's Fort, San Jose, Monterey, and Santa Cruz before settling successfully in San Jose to raise a family.

**Shaw, Reuben Cole.** Born in Massachusetts in 1826. Trained in carpenter's trade. Marries in 1847 and then journeys to California in 1851. Having little success in the gold fields, he returns to move his family on to Ohio and Iowa. He finally settles in Indiana, where he becomes a successful businessman and leading citizen. He dies in 1903.

**Shepherd, Dr. J. S.** No record.

**Thornton, J. Quinn.** Born in West Virginia in 1810. Goes to Oregon in 1846 by the new Applegate Trail. He blames Jesse Applegate personally for all the hardships of that trail, and they carry on a feud for years. He becomes active in the volatile area of Oregon politics and is very active in the creation of Oregon Territory. He serves as a judge and advocate for territorial status in Washington. He dies in 1888.

**Tinker, Charles.** Born in Ohio in 1821. He was trained as a wagon-maker. He journeys to California in 1849, leaving wife and family behind. He returns to Ohio in 1850 via the long Horn route. He goes into the manufacture of farm machinery and tools, and becomes very successful in business.

**Todd, F. W.** Todd comes to California with the Swasey-Todd Party of 1845. He settles in Sonoma in 1846 and has the distinction not only of painting the Bear Flag of the Bear Flag Rebellion but also of being captured briefly by the Californians. He leaves Sonoma to live in El Dorado County, where Todd Valley is named after him.

**Ware, Joseph E.** Ware writes his *Guide* without actually having traveled the route himself. He did it by drawing heavily on Frémont's reports and maps. His *Guide* is published in early 1849 in time for the Gold Rush and proves surprisingly good. He sets out to travel the route in 1849 but becomes quite sick and (as reported by Delano) is deserted to die alone by his companions. He is succored by others but dies a few days later.

**Wilkins, James F.** Born in London and trained as a professional artist and portrait painter. Journeys to California in 1849 from St. Louis with the idea of painting a panorama of the emigrant trail when he returned. He returns almost immediately via Panama with his sketches and goes to work. After several months of painting with assistants, his panorama opens in Peoria in 1850 and then tours to St. Louis and other cities. It seems to have enjoyed some success, but Wilkins goes back to serious painting. He dies in Illinois in 1888.

**Wistar, Isaac Jones.** Born in 1827 in Pennsylvania. He journeys to California in 1849 and then goes to work for a time for the Hudson's Bay Company in the far Northwest. He returns to California to study law. He practices in San Francisco for a time and then returns to Pennsylvania, where he raises a volunteer group called the California Regiment to fight in the Civil War.

# A PORTFOLIO OF MAPS

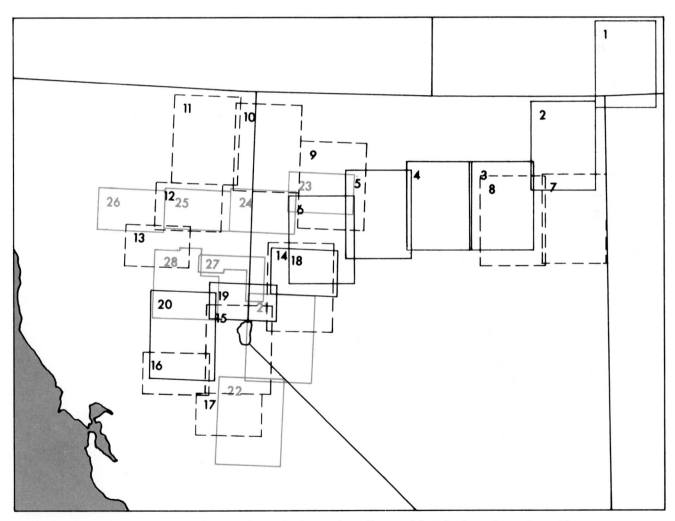

*The following maps show the actual trails used by the immigrants as they relate to present-day roads, cities, political boundaries, and major land-marks. In many cases, it can be seen, the trails can be reached easily from highways. The scale for all maps is 1:500,000, one inch equaling approximately eight miles. Key numbers indicate the sequence in the portfolio. maps*

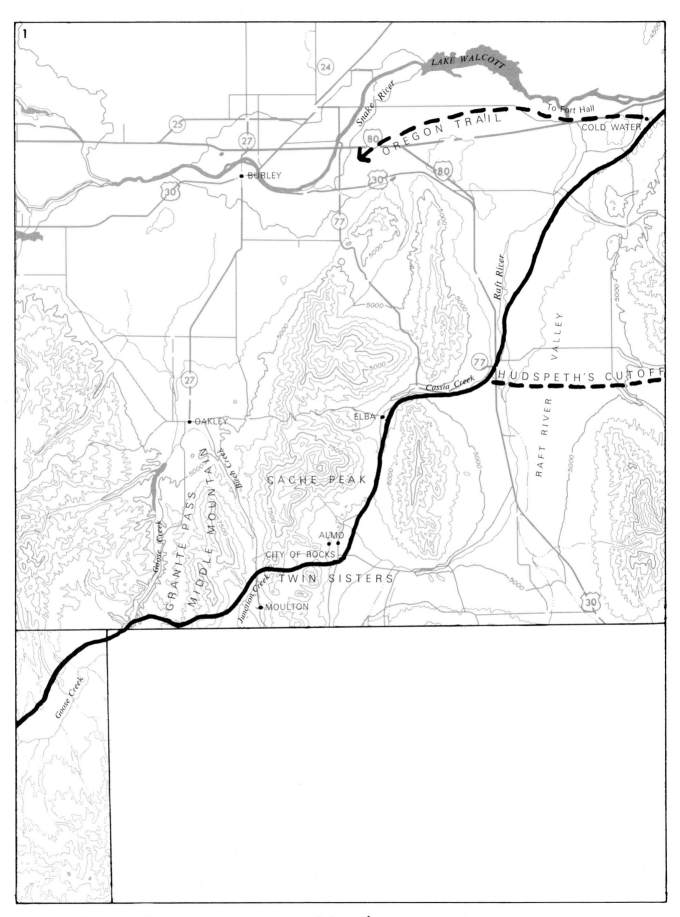

The Raft River–Humboldt Approach

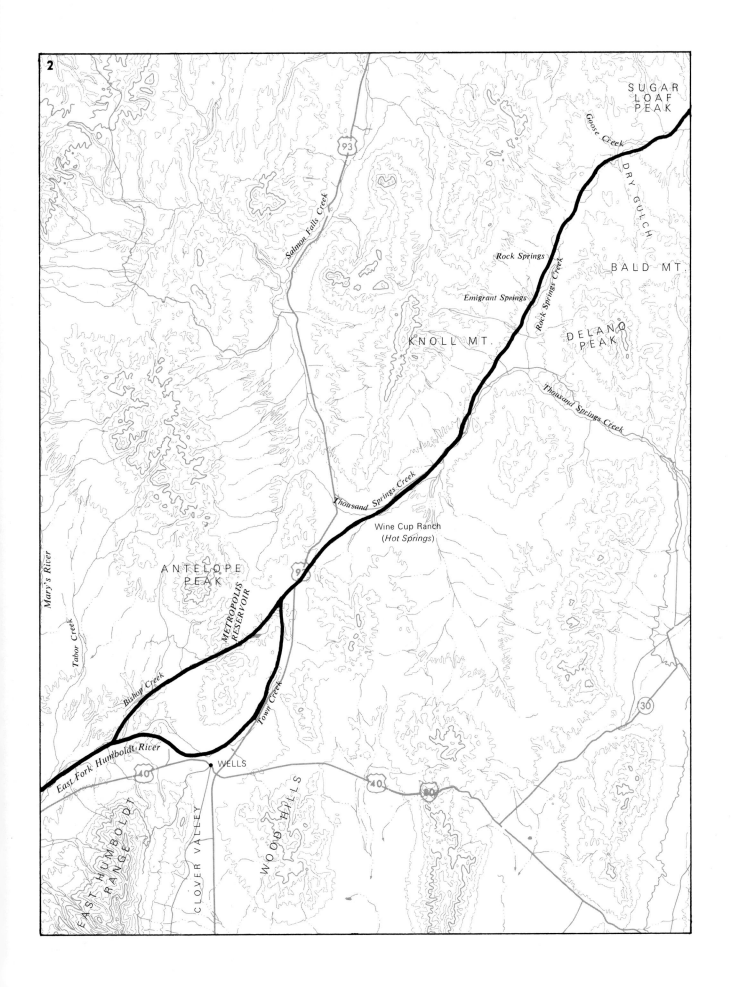

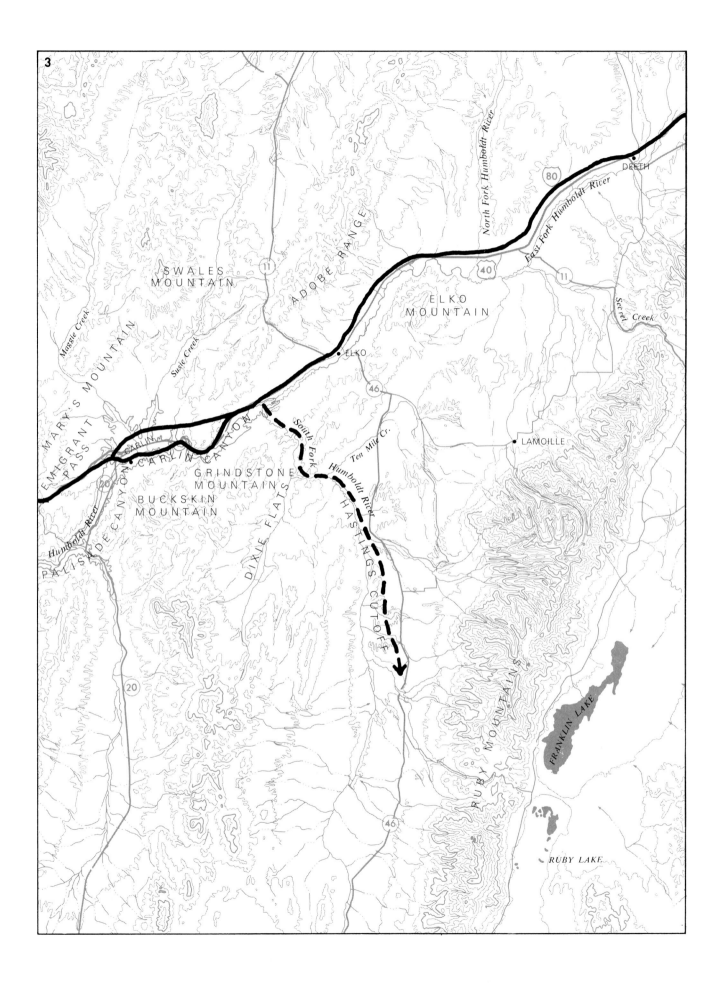

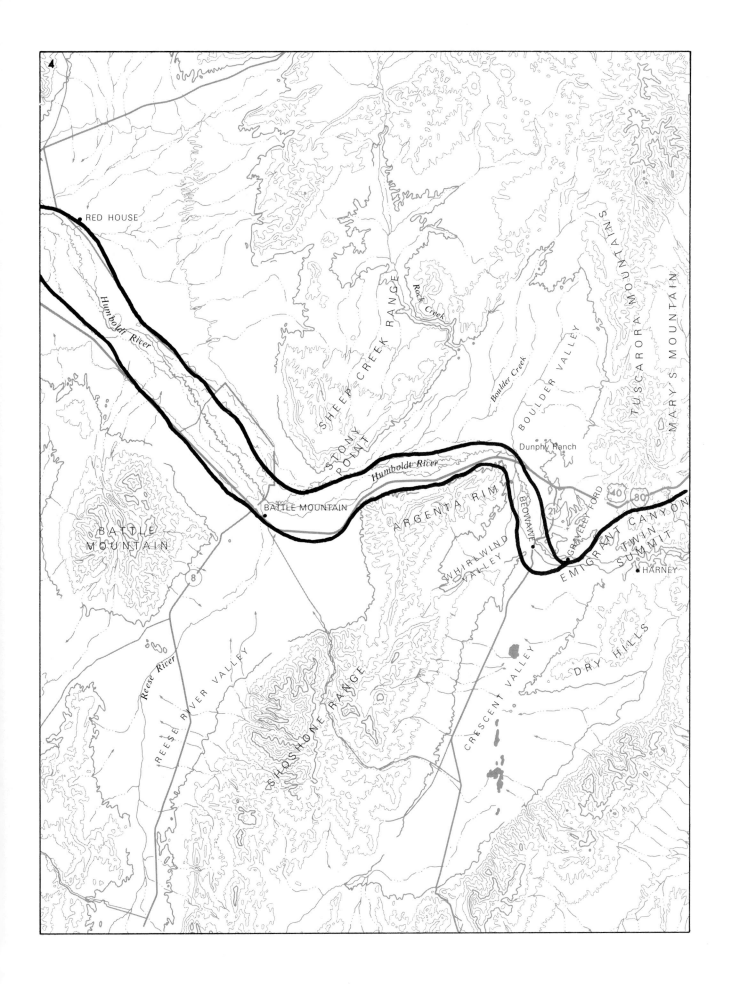

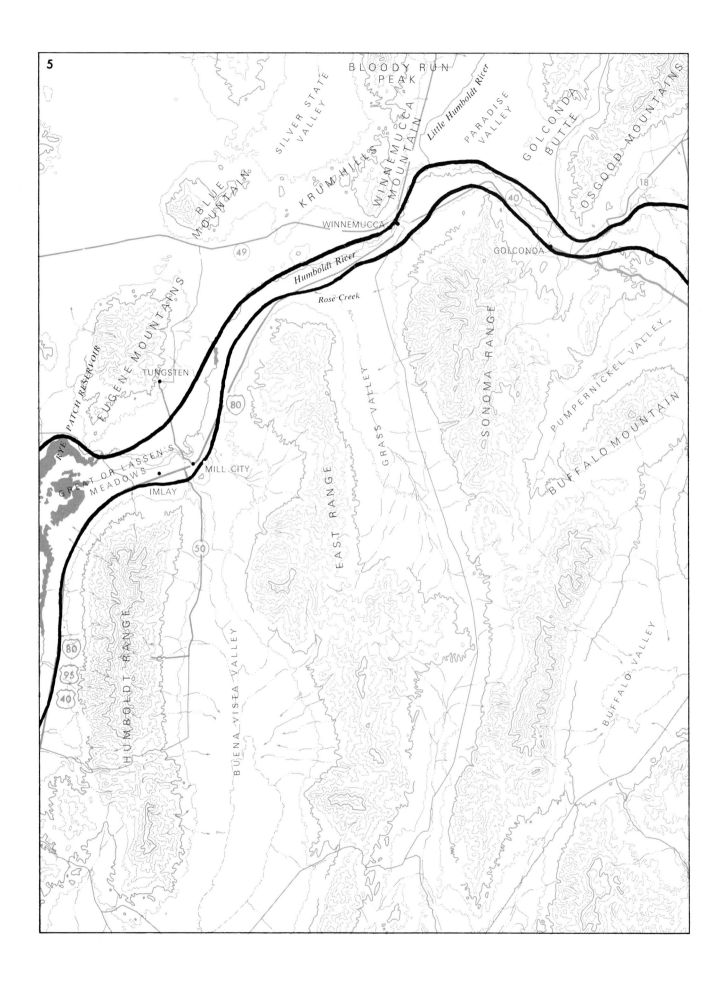

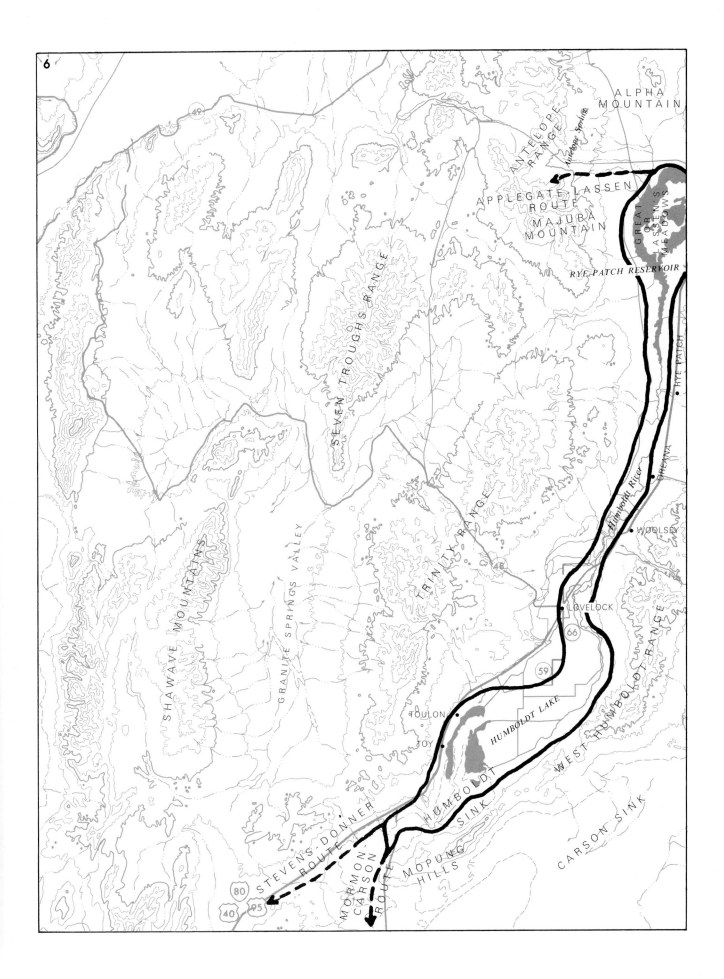

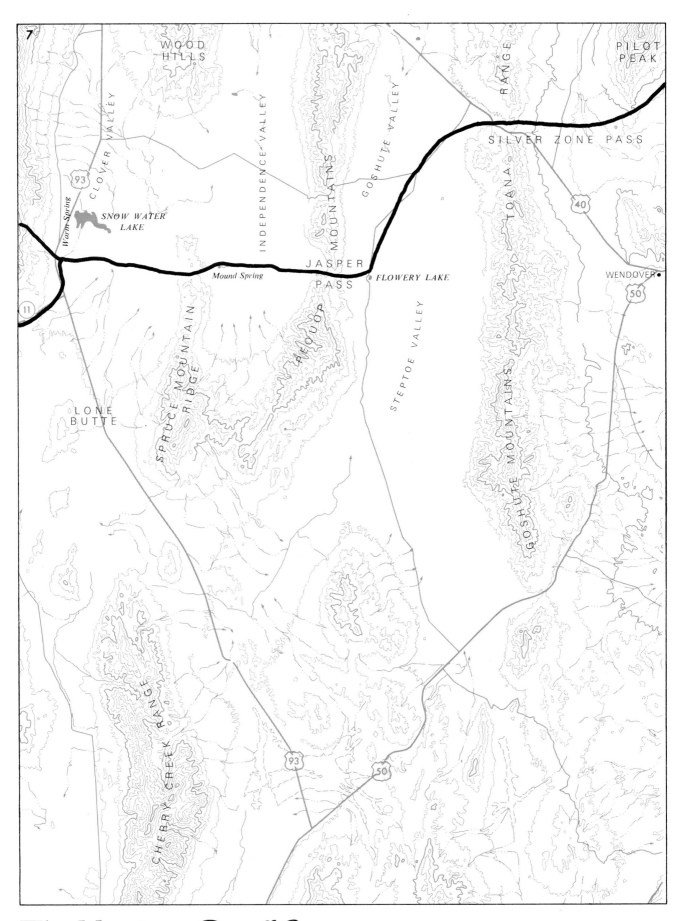

The Hastings Cutoff Route

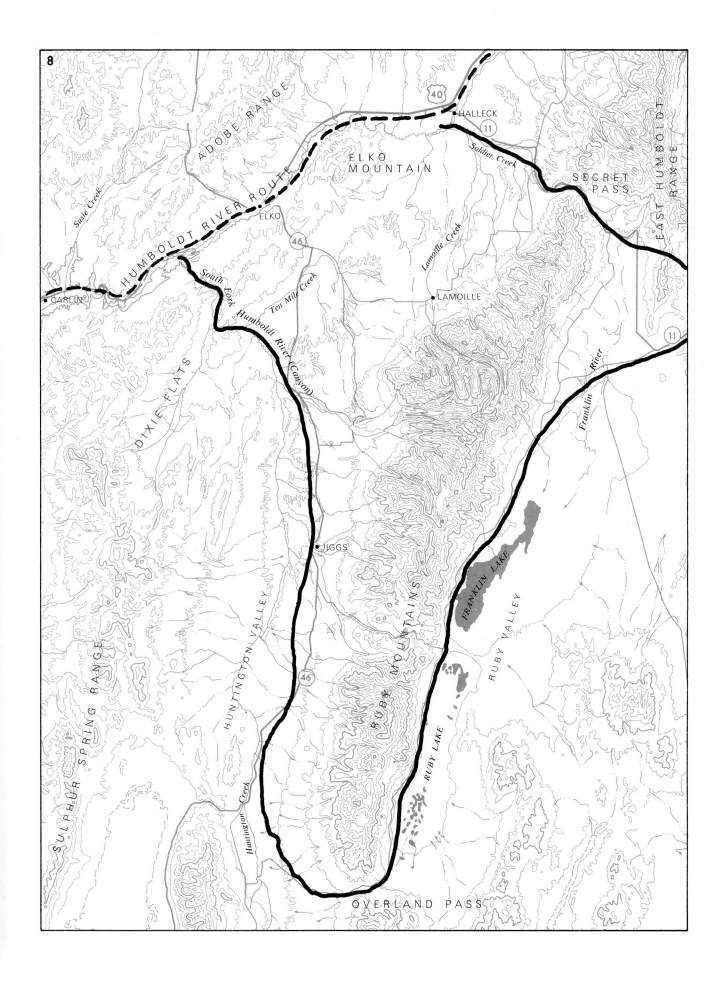

**8**

SULPHUR SPRING RANGE

ADOBE RANGE

*Susie Creek*

HUMBOLDT RIVER ROUTE

CARLIN

ELKO

ELKO MOUNTAIN

*South Fork Humboldt River (Canyon)*

*Ten Mile Creek*

*Lamoille Creek*

LAMOILLE

HALLECK

*Soldier Creek*

SECRET PASS

EAST HUMBOLDT RANGE

DIXIE FLATS

*Franklin River*

HUNTINGTON VALLEY

JIGGS

RUBY MOUNTAINS

FRANKLIN LAKE

RUBY VALLEY

*Huntington Creek*

RUBY LAKE

OVERLAND PASS

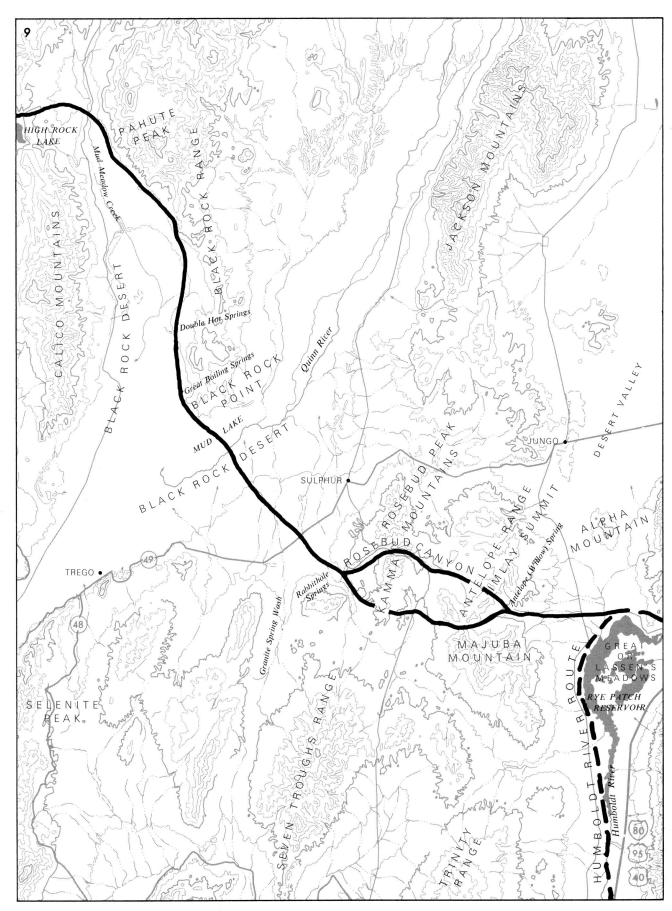

# The Applegate-Lassen Route

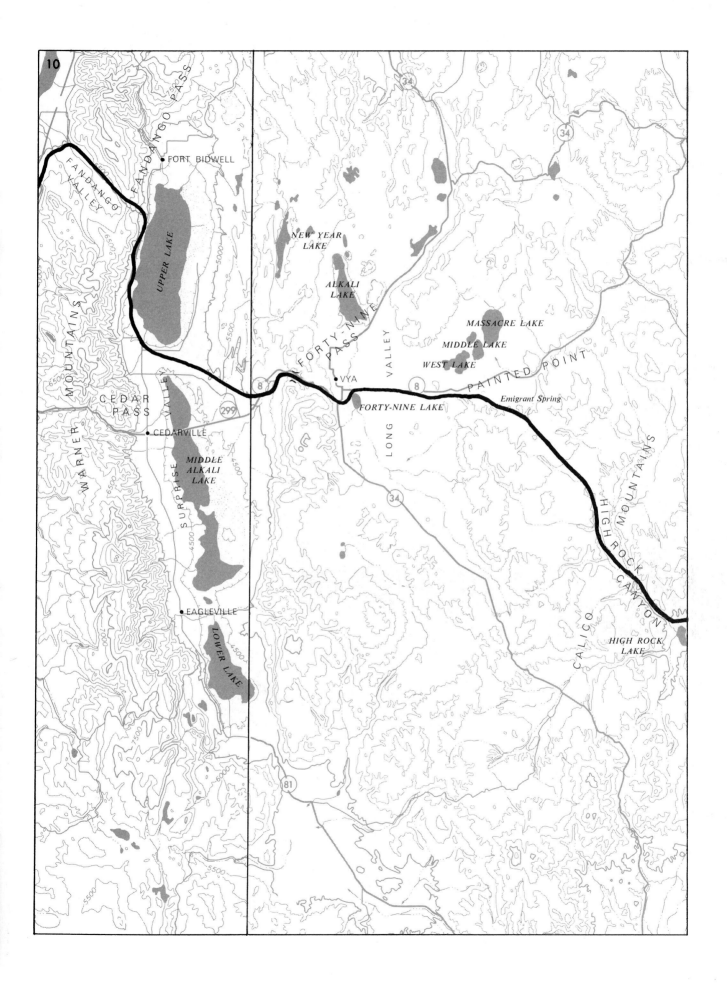

## 10

FANDANGO PASS

FORT BIDWELL

FANDANGO VALLEY

WARNER MOUNTAINS

UPPER LAKE

NEW YEAR LAKE

ALKALI LAKE

FORTY-NINE PASS

MASSACRE LAKE

MIDDLE LAKE

WEST LAKE

PAINTED POINT

CEDAR PASS

CEDARVILLE

SURPRISE VALLEY

MIDDLE ALKALI LAKE

VYA

FORTY-NINE LAKE

Emigrant Spring

LONG VALLEY

HIGH ROCK MOUNTAINS

EAGLEVILLE

LOWER LAKE

HIGH ROCK CANYON

CALICO

HIGH ROCK LAKE

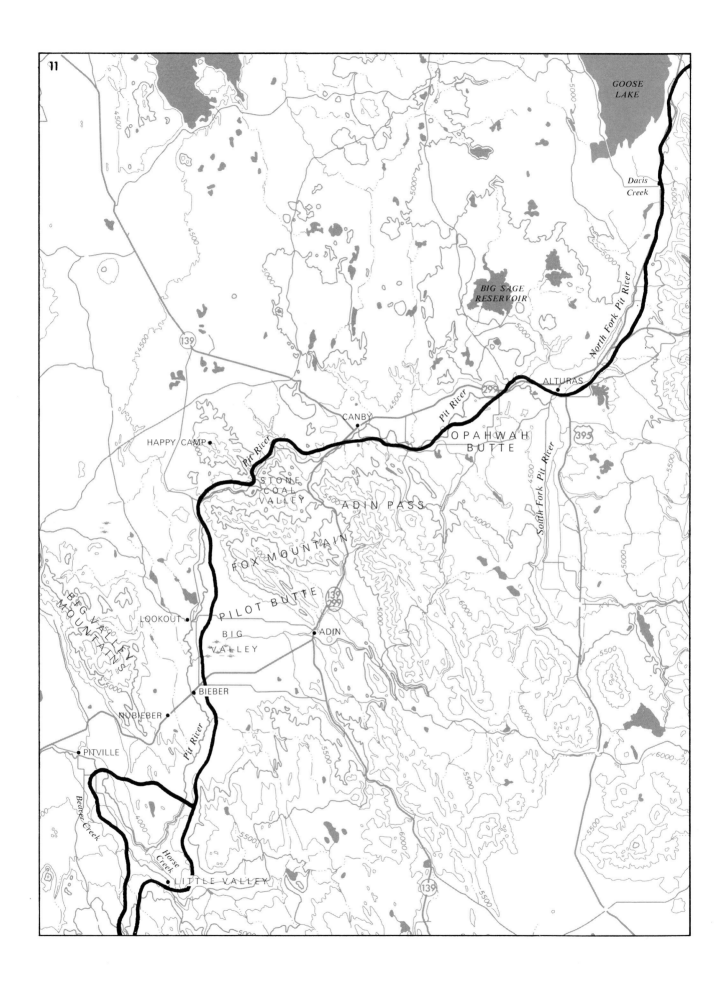

11

GOOSE
LAKE

Davis
Creek

North Fork Pit River

BIG SAGE
RESERVOIR

ALTURAS

Pit River

299

395

CANBY

OPAHWAH
BUTTE

HAPPY CAMP

Pit River

South Fork Pit River

STONE
COAL
VALLEY

ADIN PASS

FOX MOUNTAIN

PILOT BUTTE

BIG VALLEY MOUNTAINS

LOOKOUT

BIG
VALLEY

139
299

ADIN

BIEBER

Pit River

NUBIEBER

PITVILLE

Beaver Creek

139

Horse Creek

LITTLE VALLEY

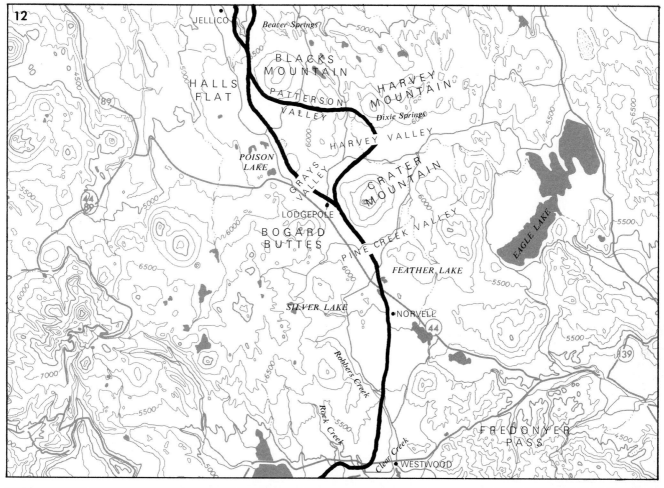

12

JELLICO
Beaver Springs
BLACKS
MOUNTAIN
HALLS
FLAT
HARVEY
MOUNTAIN
PATTERSON
VALLEY
Dixie Springs
HARVEY VALLEY
89
POISON
LAKE
GRAYS
VALLEY
CRATER
MOUNTAIN
LODGEPOLE
BOGARD
BUTTES
PINE CREEK VALLEY
EAGLE LAKE
44
FEATHER LAKE
SILVER LAKE
NORVELL
44
139
Robbers Creek
Rock Creek
FREDONYER
PASS
Clear Creek
WESTWOOD

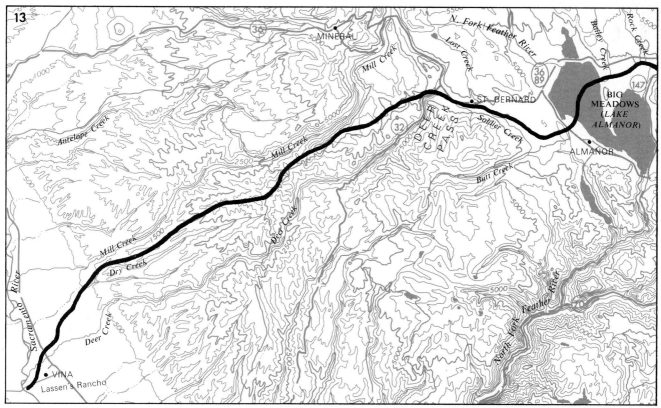

13

36
MINERAL
N. Fork Feather River
Lost Creek
Rock Creek
Butte Creek
Mill Creek
36
89
147
BIG
MEADOWS
(LAKE
ALMANOR)
ST. BERNARD
Antelope Creek
Mill Creek
32
DEER CREEK PASS
Soldier Creek
ALMANOR
Mill Creek
Deer Creek
Butt Creek
Mill Creek
Dry Creek
Deer Creek
Sacramento River
North York Feather River
VINA
Lassen's Rancho

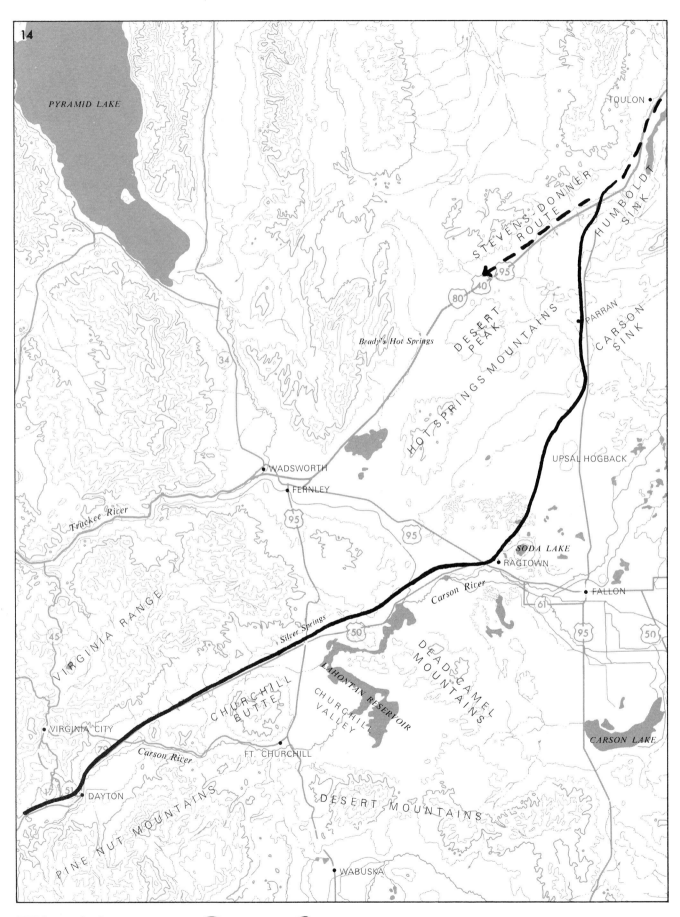

# The Mormon-Carson Route

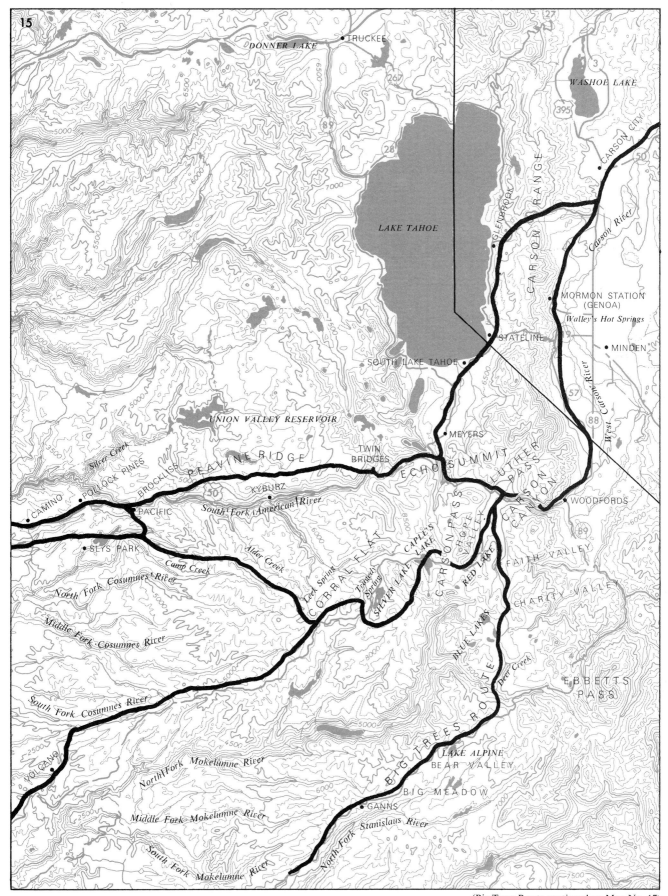

15

DONNER LAKE • TRUCKEE

6500

267

89

28

7000

WASHOE LAKE

3

395

27

CARSON CITY

50

LAKE TAHOE

GLENBROOK

CARSON RANGE

Carson River

MORMON STATION
(GENOA)

Walley's Hot Springs

STATELINE

MINDEN

SOUTH LAKE TAHOE

6500

West Carson River

MEYERS

57

88

5000

UNION VALLEY RESERVOIR

TWIN
BRIDGES

ECHO SUMMIT

LUTHER PASS

WOODFORDS

PEAVINE RIDGE

89

Silver Creek

POLLOCK PINES

BROCKLISS

KYBURZ

50

South Fork American River

CARSON PASS

HOPE VALLEY

CARSON CANYON

FAITH VALLEY

CAMINO

PACIFIC

6000

8500

CAPLE'S LAKE

RED LAKE

CHARITY VALLEY

SLYS PARK

Camp Creek

Alder Creek

Leek Spring

CORRAL FLAT

Tragedy Springs

SILVER LAKE

North Fork Cosumnes River

Middle Fork Cosumnes River

8000

BLUE LAKES

Deer Creek

EBBETTS PASS

8500

5000

South Fork Cosumnes River

4500

5000

2500

BIG TREES ROUTE

LAKE ALPINE

BEAR VALLEY

VOLCANO

North Fork Mokelumne River

6000

BIG MEADOW

GANNS

Middle Fork Mokelumne River

North Fork Stanislaus River

2500

South Fork Mokelumne River

7000

7500

(Big Trees Route continued on Map No. 17)

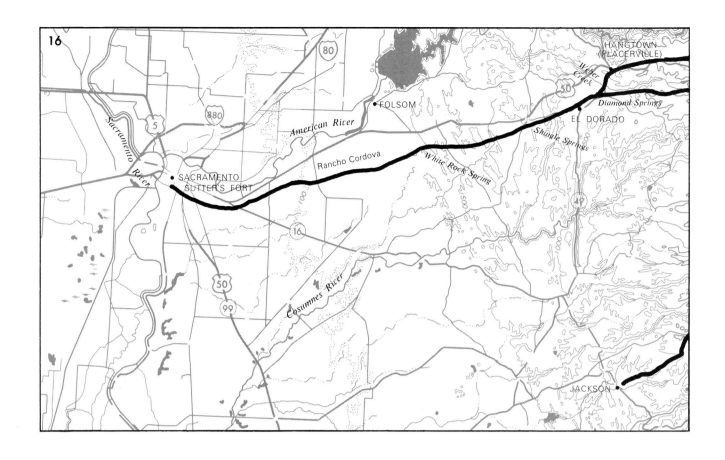

16

HANGTOWN
(PLACERVILLE)

FOLSOM

*American River*

*Sacramento River*

Rancho Cordova

SACRAMENTO
SUTTER'S FORT

*White Rock Spring*

Diamond Springs

EL DORADO

*Shingle Springs*

*Weber Creek*

*Cosumnes River*

JACKSON

(Big Trees Route continued from Map No. 15)

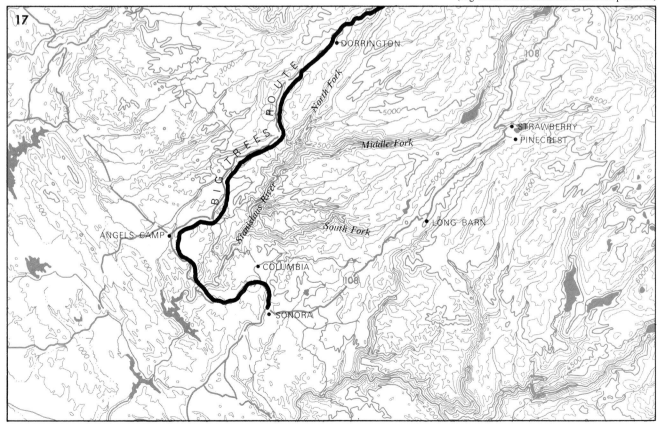

17

DORRINGTON

*North Fork*

STRAWBERRY
PINECREST

*Middle Fork*

B I G   T R E E S   R O U T E

*Stanislaus River*

*South Fork*

LONG BARN

ANGELS CAMP

COLUMBIA

SONORA

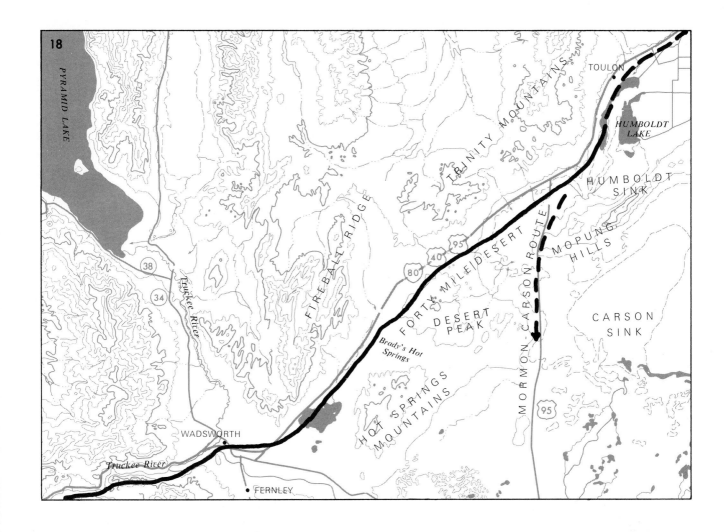

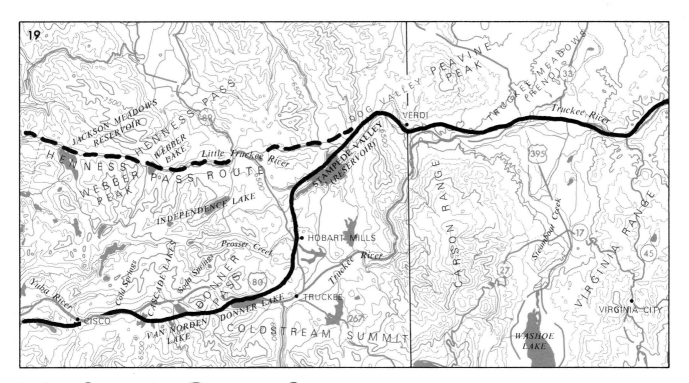

# The Stevens-Donner Route

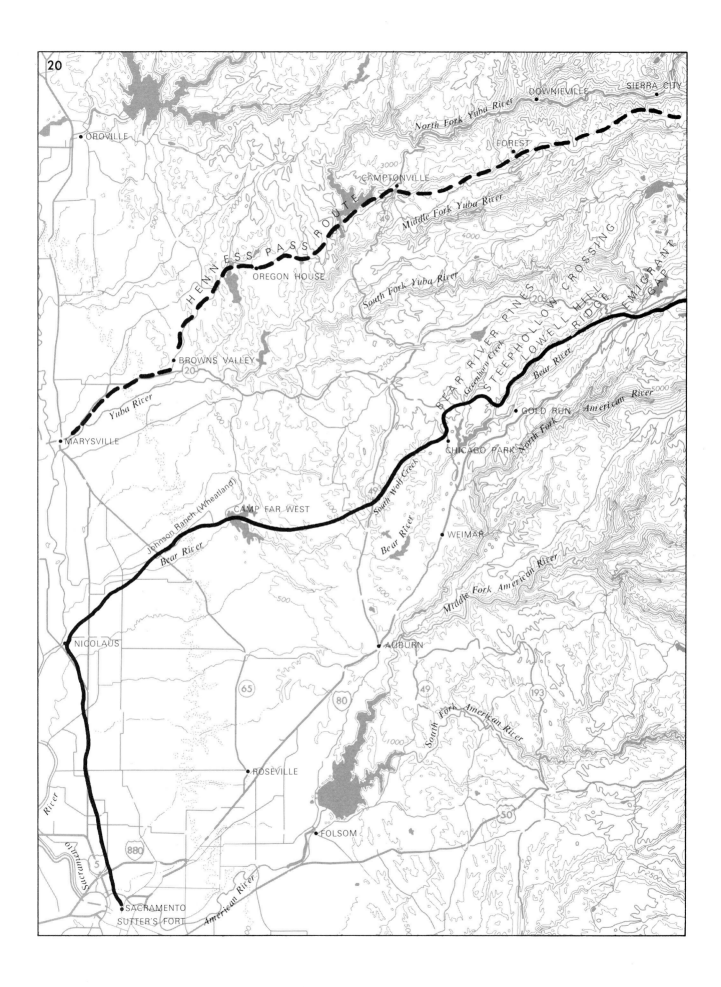

20

OROVILLE

DOWNIEVILLE          SIERRA CITY

*North Fork Yuba River*

FOREST

3000

CAMPTONVILLE

H E N N E S S   P A S S   R O U T E

*Middle Fork Yuba River*

4000

OREGON HOUSE

*South Fork Yuba River*

B E A R   R I V E R   P I N E S

S T E E P H O L L O W   C R O S S I N G

E M I G R A N T   G A P

*Greenhorn Creek*

L O W E L L   H I L L   R I D G E

20

BROWNS VALLEY

*Bear River*

20

*Yuba River*

GOLD RUN    *North Fork  American River*

5000

MARYSVILLE

CHICAGO PARK    *North Fork*

80

*South Wolf Creek*

JOHNSON RANCH (WHEATLAND)

CAMP FAR WEST

*Bear River*

WEIMAR

*Bear River*

*Middle Fork American River*

3000

*River*

NICOLAUS

AUBURN

65

80

49

193

3500

*South Fork American River*

1000

ROSEVILLE

50

*River*

FOLSOM

880

5

SACRAMENTO

SUTTER'S FORT

*American River*

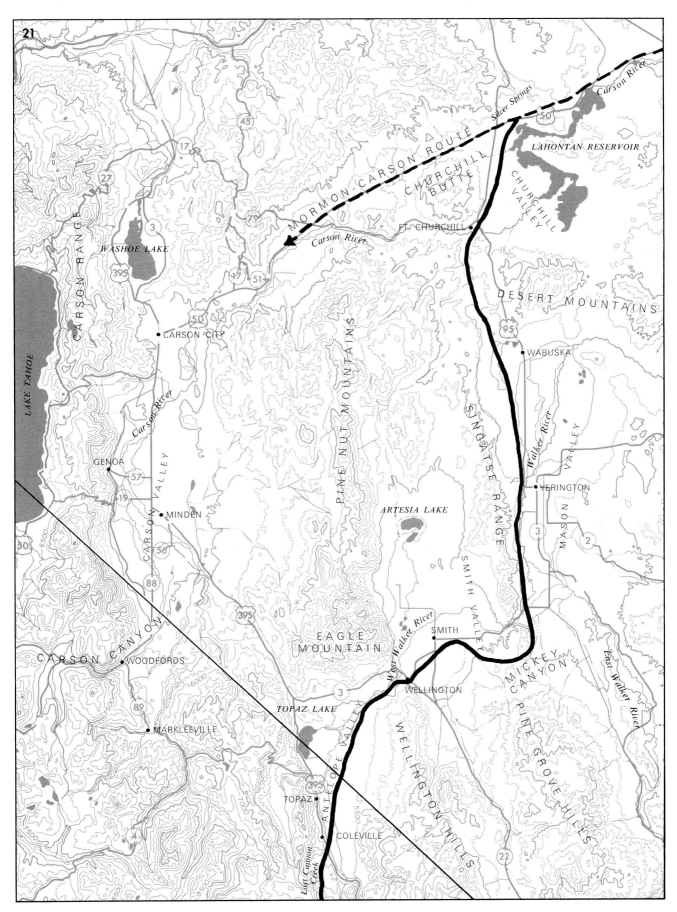

## 21

LAKE TAHOE

CARSON RANGE

WASHOE LAKE

27

45

17

3

395

*Carson River*

MORMON-CARSON ROUTE

*Silver Springs*

CHURCHILL BUTTE

FT. CHURCHILL

*Carson River*

LAHONTAN RESERVOIR

50

CHURCHILL VALLEY

DESERT MOUNTAINS

17 51

50

CARSON CITY

GENOA

57

19

MINDEN

56

88

80

395

CARSON VALLEY

*Carson River*

PINE NUT MOUNTAINS

ARTESIA LAKE

SINGATSE RANGE

95

WABUSKA

*Walker River*

YERINGTON

MASON VALLEY

3

2

EAGLE MOUNTAIN

3

*West Walker River*

SMITH

WELLINGTON

SMITH VALLEY

MICKEY CANYON

*East Walker River*

CARSON CANYON

WOODFORDS

89

MARKLEEVILLE

TOPAZ LAKE

ANTELOPE VALLEY

*West Walker River*

WELLINGTON HILLS

PINE GROVE HILLS

TOPAZ

COLEVILLE

*Lost Cannon Creek*

395

22

# The Sonora Route

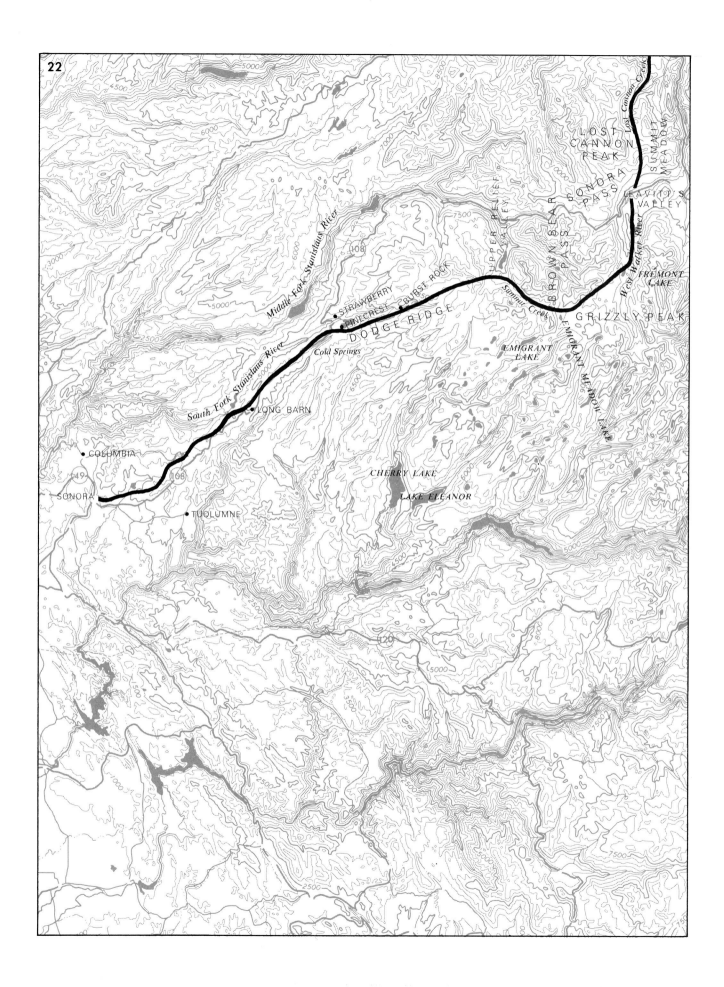

22

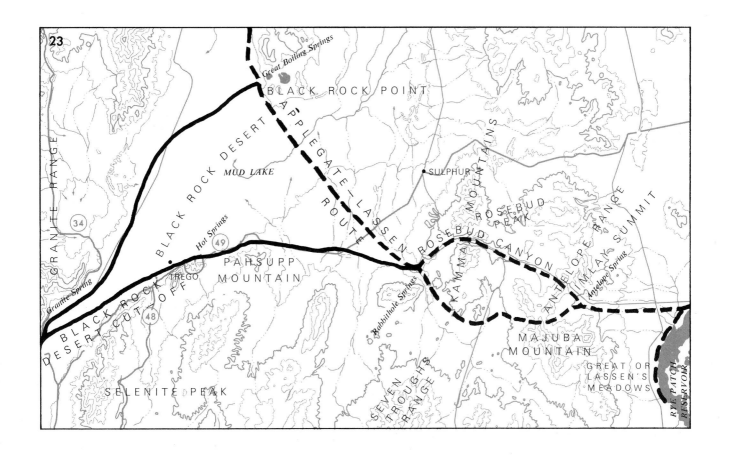

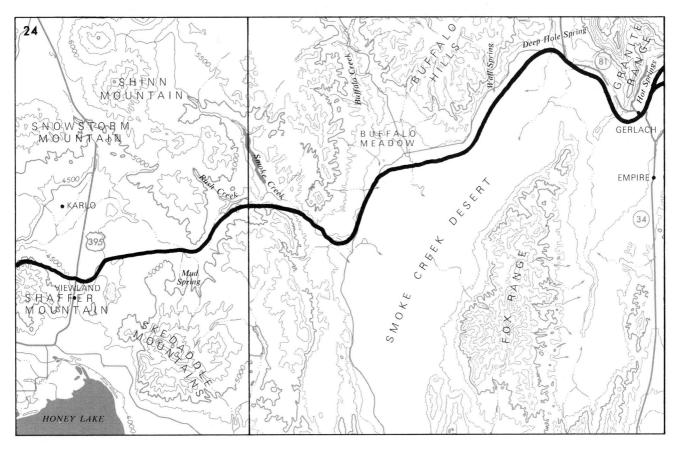

# The Nobles' Route

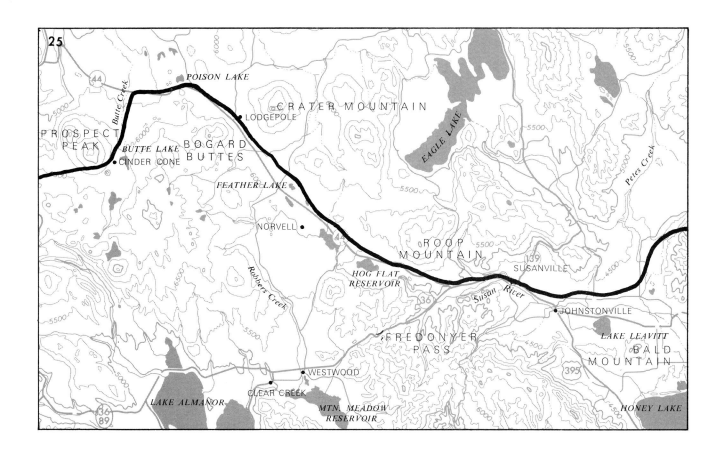

25

POISON LAKE

44

Butte Creek

CRATER MOUNTAIN

LODGEPOLE

EAGLE LAKE

Petes Creek

PROSPECT
PEAK

BUTTE LAKE

CINDER CONE

BOGARD
BUTTES

FEATHER LAKE

5500

NORVELL

44

ROOP
MOUNTAIN

5500

SUSANVILLE

139

Robbers Creek

HOG FLAT
RESERVOIR

JOHNSTONVILLE

Susan River

36

5500

FREDONYER
PASS

LAKE LEAVITT

BALD
MOUNTAIN

395

WESTWOOD

5500

136
89

LAKE ALMANOR

CLEAR CREEK

MTN. MEADOW
RESERVOIR

HONEY LAKE

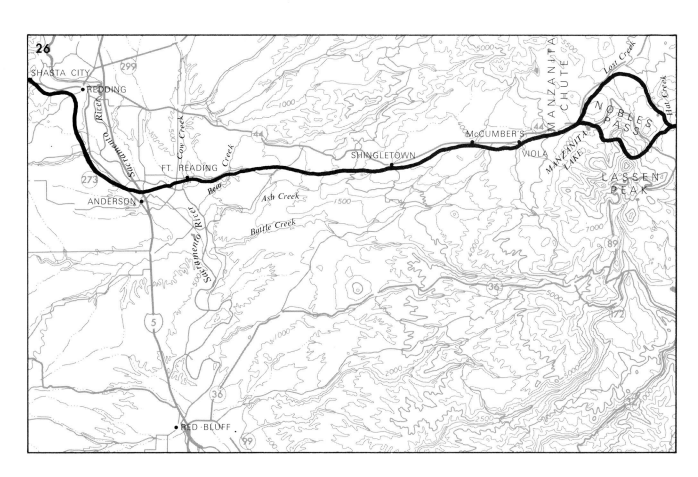

26

SHASTA CITY

299

REDDING

MANZANITA
CHUTE

Lost Creek

Hat Creek

NOBLES
PASS

Sacramento River

Cow Creek

44

McCUMBER'S

VIOLA

MANZANITA
LAKE

FT. READING

Bear Creek

SHINGLETOWN

Clear Creek

273

LASSEN
PEAK

ANDERSON

Sacramento River

Ash Creek

1500

7000

Battle Creek

89

5

4000

36

172

36

1000

5000

2500

RED BLUFF

99

2000

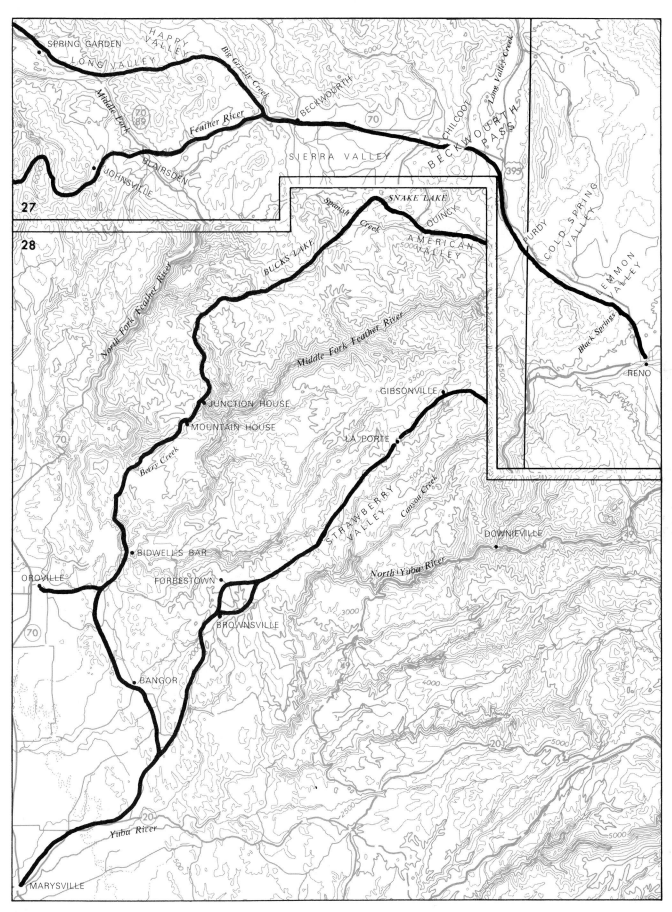

# The Beckwourth Route

# INDEX

*Handwritten:* 8/1976 — From: San Ramon Valley Republican Women's Club Steak Bar-B-Que.

*Handwritten:* Rosemary Ramsey, Chairman

(*Page numbers in italic type indicate illustrations.*)